WHEN THE WORST HAPPENS

EXTRAORDINARY STORIES OF SURVIVAL

TANYA LLOYD KYI
ART BY DAVID PARKINS

annick press
toronto + new york + vancouver

*TO MIN, JULIA, AND MATTHEW, WHO WOULD MAKE
ANY DESERT ISLAND ENTERTAINING —TLK*

*FOR SUE AND ROB, WHO RESCUED US AGAIN ON
CHRISTMAS DAY. FIND FRIENDS! —DP*

© 2014 Tanya Lloyd Kyi (text)
© 2014 David Parkins (illustrations)

Edited by Alison Kooistra
Copyedited by Catherine Marjoribanks
Proofread by Tanya Trafford
Designed by Natalie Olsen/Kisscut Design

Annick Press Ltd.

We acknowledge the support of the Canada Council for the Arts, the Ontario Arts
Council, and the Government of Canada through the Canada Book Fund (CBF) for our
publishing activities.

ONTARIO ARTS COUNCIL
CONSEIL DES ARTS DE L'ONTARIO

50 YEARS OF ONTARIO GOVERNMENT SUPPORT OF THE ARTS
50 ANS DE SOUTIEN DU GOUVERNEMENT DE L'ONTARIO AUX ARTS

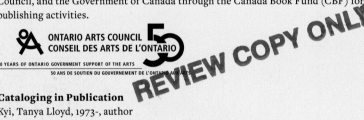

Cataloging in Publication
Kyi, Tanya Lloyd, 1973-, author
When the worst happens : extraordinary stories of survival /
by Tanya Lloyd Kyi ; artwork by David Parkins.

Includes bibliographical references and index.
ISBN 978-1-55451-682-7 (pbk.).—ISBN 978-1-55451-683-4 (bound)

1. Survival—Juvenile literature. I. Parkins, David illustrator   II. Title.

G525.K95 2014   j613.6'9   C2014-900391-9

Distributed in Canada by:	**Published in the U.S.A. by Annick Press (U.S.) Ltd.**
Firefly Books Ltd.	Distributed in the U.S.A. by:
50 Staples Avenue, Unit 1	Firefly Books (U.S.) Inc.
Richmond Hill, ON L4B 0A7	P.O. Box 1338
	Ellicott Station
	Buffalo, NY 14205

Printed in China

Visit us at: **www.annickpress.com**
Visit Tanya Lloyd Kyi at: **www.tanyalloydkyi.com**
Visit David Parkins at: **www.davidparkins.com**

Also available in e-book format.
Please visit **www.annickpress.com/ebooks.html**
for more details. Or scan

CONTENTS

THE
BIG
"WHAT IF?"

Where are you sitting as you read these words? Probably, you're in a warm and comfortable spot, breathing plentiful air. Maybe you have a drink or a snack nearby.

JULIANE KOEPCKE, AGE 17, PERU

What if one minute you were safely buckled into your airplane seat, and the next minute your chair was free-falling through the sky as the jungle trees grew terrifyingly closer, sharper, and harder?

BALA NONA, AGE 12, TORRES STRAIT
(body of water between Australia and New Guinea)

What if you and your family were on your way to a birthday party when your boat capsized in the ocean?

JIMMY SANCHEZ, AGE 19, CHILE

What if your workplace was a mine 212 stories below the ground?
What if one day the mountain exploded around you, trapping you
in darkness?

PUNNY EBIERBING, AGE 8, ICE FLOE,
Arctic Ocean off the coast of Greenland

What if your mother and father were part of an expedition to find
the North Pole? What if one day your ship floated away and left you
stranded and starving on a floating chunk of ice?

In the coming pages, you'll find these four stories and many others—stories about people grappling with all sorts of extreme environments. In some of these places, people did mind-boggling things to survive. They ate bugs, drank from puddles, fought off hungry predators, performed emergency surgery, wrapped themselves in seaweed, and crawled down a mountain with a broken leg. They scratched their way out of piles of rubble, staggered through deserts, and faced the emptiness of space. But in other places, people lost hope. They sat and waited for death.

So what makes the difference between life and death? A strange mix of mental strategies, survival skills, and sheer luck allows some people to find their way back to civilization, even when it seems impossible.

What are the secrets to their success?

And there's one other question, of course . . .

What would *you* do to survive?

THE KEY TO SURVIVAL

Watch for these icons throughout the book. They mark places where people use great survival strategies . . . and places where they go astray. A red icon means someone is doing the opposite of what experts recommend.

FIND FRIENDS

The key to many emergency situations is finding people who can help you get home—they might be professional rescuers or local inhabitants.

ACT!

To avoid panic and stay focused, get both your brain and body in gear. You need to make plans and take action. Sometimes it doesn't even matter *what* you do. As long as you are doing something, you can keep yourself alert, calm, and hopeful.

GO BACK TO BASICS

What do I have, what can I find, and how long will it last? To survive, you need to stay warm and dry. You need air, water, food, and rest. The sooner you find these things, the better.

USE YOUR KNOW-HOW

If I eat it, will I die? Understanding the dangers and the resources of your environment is a major advantage. A few basic skills, like how to light a fire or use a compass, can also make a huge difference.

KEEP YOUR COOL

Survival situations are seriously stressful. If you can turn fear or anger into motivation, you might find the strength to persevere. Stay confident and think positively.

GET ZEN

Finding a way to keep your mind focused is critical. Some people pray, chant, or repeat words and patterns to themselves. Others breathe rhythmically or meditate. These activities tell your mind that you're in control and things are going to be okay.

PLAY NICE

If you're stranded with other people, communication and empathy are key. Crises are solved more quickly when groups work together; if people can't get along, things get more dangerous for everyone. Plus, caring for others can turn you from a victim into a rescuer. It can give you a feeling of purpose and increase your motivation to survive.

Many of the people in the following chapters used these strategies well. Others went astray—and paid a terrible price!

In the first chapter, you'll learn about how our bodies and minds react to emergencies. Sometimes, people take immediate action and handle danger as if they were professional stunt artists. Other times, they act more like petrified animals! Our brains are wired in fascinating ways.

In Chapter 2, there are stories of survivors who faced the most extreme environments on—and off—the planet. You'll read about the strange things people do to meet their basic human needs, and how they react when water's not available at the twist of a tap and food doesn't appear with the pull of a refrigerator handle.

Chapter 3 is all about the emotional challenges people face when they're torn from their cozy lives and dropped into unfamiliar and frightening places. Some have to dig for the inner strength to face these situations alone; others have to find ways to work with (or around) difficult companions.

In Chapter 4, tough situations get even tougher. Sharks, anyone? Piranhas? Blizzards? Spacesuit malfunctions? Or maybe you'd like an open wound with your survival scenario? A little fear can keep people alert and motivated, but too much can send them into mental meltdown. In these situations, people have to learn how to control their racing hearts and swirling thoughts.

Finally, Chapter 5 explores the experiences people have if and when they actually manage to return to real life. Going home is often not the end of a survivor's troubles—sometimes, it's just the beginning.

But you don't have to read this book chapter by chapter. If you want to, you can jump around all over the place! There are four major survival tales told in these pages—Juliane's, Bala's, Jimmy's, and Punny's. When one part of a story ends, you can skip ahead to that story's installment in the next chapter to find out what happens next.

If you want, you can even read the final chapter first. You'd miss all the maggot-infested, hallucination-inducing, lion-evading fun. But you would find out once and for all . . . what happens when people survive the unsurvivable.

CHAPTER 1

SURVIVOR

101

A squirrel scampers halfway across a busy road. Then, as headlights bear down, the animal freezes. It can't go backward. It can't go forward. It simply stares, wide-eyed, at approaching death.

You'd think, with our bigger brains, we could deal with danger better than a rodent. But it turns out that squirrels and humans have quite a bit in common when it comes to handling crises.

FIGHT OR FLIGHT OR FREEZE

IN THE LATE 1800s, a scientist named Walter Bradford Cannon was studying digestion using newly developed x-ray technology. He kept having to pause his observations when people's stomachs stopped moving for a while, then restarted. Eventually, he noticed that these stops and starts happened whenever there was a loud noise nearby, or a surprising movement.

But why would sudden noises affect the stomach?

By 1906, Walter had moved on to the study of nerves, looking for a way to explain this startle response. He began investigating a specialized set of nerves called the sympathetic nervous system, which seemed to "activate" the body and get it ready to deal with stressful situations. In the 1930s, Walter coined the phrase "fight or flight response."

Recently, some scientists have renamed this the "fight or flight or freeze response." It describes the way our bodies are wired to deal with emergencies. If you're crossing the road, just like that squirrel, and headlights swerve toward you, here's what happens beneath your skin:

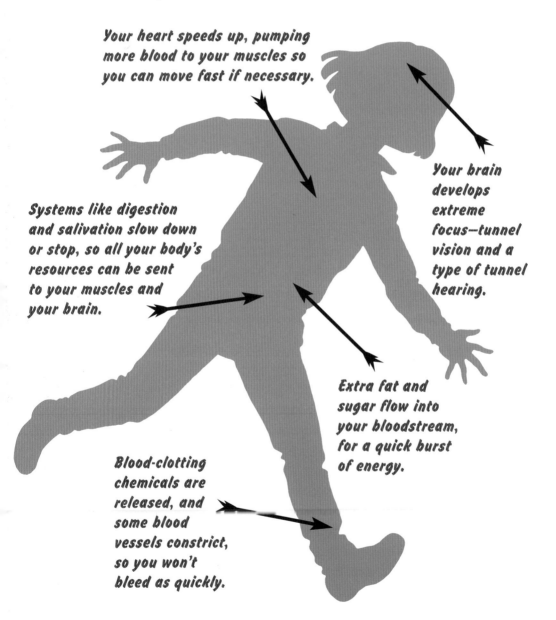

Your heart speeds up, pumping more blood to your muscles so you can move fast if necessary.

Systems like digestion and salivation slow down or stop, so all your body's resources can be sent to your muscles and your brain.

Your brain develops extreme focus—tunnel vision and a type of tunnel hearing.

Extra fat and sugar flow into your bloodstream, for a quick burst of energy.

Blood-clotting chemicals are released, and some blood vessels constrict, so you won't bleed as quickly.

All these reactions are designed to help you deal with danger, by running away, facing it head on, or by freezing— hiding, or playing dead.

In the modern world, "flight" is often the best answer. Obviously if there's a car speeding toward you, you're going to race across the road, not stay to fight. But our hard-wiring makes more sense when you think about what humans have to face when they live in close contact with nature, as most of us did for thousands of years, and some of us still do today. If you're walking through the jungle, and a tiger leaps out, your fight or flight or freeze response prepares you to either battle the animal or run for your life.

And how would you feel if you were suddenly dropped into a jungle with jaguars, snakes, spiders, and flesh-eating fish? Some quick reactions might be helpful!

That actually happened to Juliane Koepcke. She was 17 years old, traveling with her mother on a flight over Peru. Then, with a deafening crack, her plane tore apart and she found herself falling.

ALONE IN THE AMAZON

IT WAS DECEMBER 24, 1971, and 17-year-old Juliane and her mother were on their way from Lima to Pucallpa, Peru, to spend Christmas with Juliane's father. Both her parents worked to preserve South America's rainforest. Her mother was an ornithologist—an expert on birds—and her zoologist father studied the region's wildlife.

To reach their research station in the Amazon jungle, Juliane and her mother would have to fly for an hour, then make the rest of the trip along rutted roads and swollen rivers. But the long journey would be worth it if they could all be together for Christmas.

The flight began like any other. Safety demonstration. Snacks. Cleanup. Then the plane flew into a thunderstorm. As the entire vessel shook, Christmas presents and purses flew from the overhead bins. From the corner of her eye, Juliane saw a blinding flash over the wing. Lightning strike, or explosion? There was no time to wonder. With a crack, the entire craft broke apart and Juliane was flung into the sky, still strapped to her row of seats. She fell from 3,000 meters (10,000 feet), awake and alert just long enough to notice the shapes of the trees growing more and more distinct below her.

The world record for surviving a fall without a parachute is held by Vesna Vulović. In 1972, the 22-year-old flight attendant fell 10,160 meters (33,330 feet) after an explosion ripped her plane apart. Though she broke her skull, her back, and her legs, she eventually recovered—and continued to fly.

Juliane regained consciousness on the rainforest floor. The bones in her shoulder felt as if they were overlapping and her right eye was swollen shut, but she was almost too dazed to fully feel the pain of her injuries. She was wearing only a sundress and one sandal. There was no one else in sight.

She was alone in the jungle.

The same storm that had torn her plane apart was pounding down on the Amazon. Soaked and shivering, Juliane pulled herself toward the upside-down airplane seats and crawled beneath them. There, she huddled in the darkness, waiting for day. And wondering . . . her mother had been in the seat beside her. And there had been other passengers on the plane, and a pilot. What had happened to them?

Can Juliane survive the rainforest on her own? Turn to page 38 to find out.

BRAIN FREEZE

IN THE MOVIES, people in dangerous situations go crazy. They race through trees, branches whipping their cheeks. Or they disintegrate into hysterics, screaming and weeping.

In reality, surprisingly few people panic. But the rest aren't necessarily much better off. In an unfamiliar situation, with fear choking their thoughts, they often find themselves incapable of useful action.

After studying plane crashes, scientists have found that one of the main delays to evacuation is that some people stay frozen in their seats. Other passengers could reach the rescue chutes more quickly if they didn't have to climb over petrified lumps. Survivors of shipwrecks and fires say the same thing—more people would be able to escape if everyone just moved. Researcher John Leach is a survival expert who has spent years studying disaster situations, and the people caught in them. He has divided humanity into three groups:

Group A is supercool. These people, about 10 to 20 percent of us, stay calm and reasonable in a crisis. They'll figure out what's going on, and take action.

Group B is stunned. About three-quarters of people are so shocked they barely move. They say they feel nothing, but their heart rates are skyrocketing. They sweat, tremble, feel nauseated, and sometimes even poop their pants.

Group C is panicked. This small percentage of people—about 10 to 15 percent—lose all ability to cope. They scream, cry, or become paralyzed with fear.

If you ever find yourself in an emergency situation with a group, you might see examples of all three reaction styles. Hopefully, you'll be the supercool one! But even then, survival isn't easy.

In 1982, on a small inflatable dinghy in the middle of the ocean, five people struggled to endure, hoping their Mayday call to the U.S. Coast Guard would bring a rescue ship. Two tried to stay cool, one was stunned, and two gave in to panic . . .

LOST AT SEA

DEBBIE'S FRIEND BRAD shook her awake, screaming at her to move. As soon as Debbie sat up, she saw why: water was crashing through the portholes and flooding the cabin. The yacht was going down.

Twenty-four-year-old Debbie Kiley was supposed to be sailing the *Trashman* from Maine to Florida, but the trip had been a disaster since the beginning. Three of her fellow sailors—John, Mark, and Meg—were constantly drunk. Now, the engine had failed, the yacht was sinking, and everyone was screaming at each other as they struggled to launch a small dinghy.

Every time they climbed aboard the life raft, the waves flipped it. For hours they clung to the side. Meg's leg had been sliced open in the race to flee the yacht; she was in shock and losing blood. Mark and John were angry and unreasonable. They finally managed to climb aboard only once the waters below them were teeming with sharks.

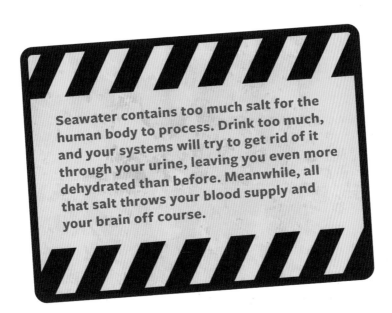

Seawater contains too much salt for the human body to process. Drink too much, and your systems will try to get rid of it through your urine, leaving you even more dehydrated than before. Meanwhile, all that salt throws your blood supply and your brain off course.

Over the days that followed, Debbie covered herself with seaweed to help her skin retain its moisture and block some of the blazing rays of the sun. Her friend Brad concentrated on catching fish. But Meg's injured leg became infected. On the fourth day, Meg sank into unconsciousness. She died that night.

In the meantime, John and Mark were so thirsty that they drank seawater. They became so dehydrated that they began hallucinating and left the boat to swim for an imaginary shore. Debbie was horrified as she heard the sharks attack her companions, but she closed her eyes and repeated the Lord's Prayer to keep herself from panicking.

On October 28, 1982, a Russian freighter spotted the dinghy and pulled two survivors on board. Debbie and Brad were the only ones to live through the five days at sea.

LEADING QUESTIONS

SO WHAT MAKES SOME PEOPLE SUPERCOOL while others panic? Well, it might be genetics. Many scientists believe that people who have a larger hippocampus—a seahorse-shaped organ in the center of the base of your brain—deal better with fear. But it's also practice. If you've overcome challenges in the past, you'll be better able to deal with new crises. Statistically, soldiers and police officers cope well in emergency situations. So do firefighters and nurses—people who are trained to leap into action and help save lives.

You don't have to be a trained professional to take charge in a crisis, but you do need to sound as though you're in control. Studies conducted by Virgin Blue Airlines and the Australian government found that when flight crews gave passengers calm, polite instructions, they were ignored. The passengers acted as if the crew members weren't there at all. But if the crew gave short, assertive instructions with firm hand gestures, passengers followed directions. They recognized and responded to strong leadership.

In 2009, a passenger plane leaving New York's LaGuardia Airport flew into a flock of geese, damaging both engines. Captain Chesley Sullenberger quickly discussed the situation with air traffic control, conferred with his copilot, then decided to crash-land in the Hudson River. After informing the passengers, he landed in the water and directed the evacuation of the plane, even walking through the aircraft twice to ensure every passenger had escaped.

Captain Sullenberger had flown for U.S. Airways for twenty-nine years; before that, he had been an air force pilot. His experience, his decisive manner in the midst of a crisis, and his ability to work closely with his coworkers helped save all the passengers on board.

Often, strong leadership can make all the difference between life and death. When one person takes charge and stays calm, that keeps everyone focused and safe. Nineteen-year-old Jimmy Sanchez and the other miners trapped in a cave-in at Chile's San José gold and copper mine were lucky to have just such a leader.

DEEP BENEATH THE EARTH

NINETEEN-YEAR-OLD JIMMY SANCHEZ worried every time he worked another shift at the San José gold and copper mine in Chile. Sometimes he'd see rockslides and small collapses in the tunnels. And he knew that the mine had only a small budget for safety precautions. Still, he felt he had to go—he needed the money to support his girlfriend and their newborn baby.

Jimmy's worst nightmare came true when a massive cave-in ripped through the mine on August 5, 2010. Rockfalls sent blasts of air rocketing through the tunnels, throwing men to the ground or forcing them against the walls. Some ran uphill, hoping for escape, only to find their routes blocked. Eventually,

they all scrambled to the very bottom of the mine, where there was a steel refuge chamber set into the stone. There, along with thirty-two other miners, Jimmy found himself trapped. He was 212 stories below ground.

It took three hours for the dust to settle enough to see. Once they'd gathered themselves and assessed the situation, the miners tried climbing to safety through the ventilation shafts, but missing ladders and further cave-ins made escape impossible. So they concentrated on surviving as well as possible within their narrow confines.

Under the direction of 54-year-old supervisor Luis Urzúa, Jimmy and the other men took stock. When they found an emergency food cache, Luis persuaded them to agree to strict rations. The food was meant to last for two days, but the miners knew they could be trapped for much longer.

For water, the men had barrels of dirty fluid meant for the machinery, and they found a place within the tunnel system where liquid was dripping and collecting. They powered up a bulldozer to dig a trench, and that allowed them to collect the water and ensure a lasting supply. Finally, the miners agreed to conserve their headlamps and the vehicle headlights, using them in shifts and as sparingly as possible.

As the days passed, and then weeks, Luis encouraged the men to stay strong, have faith, and accept whatever outcome occurred. With no way to escape on their own, their only hope was that rescuers would find them.

Seven hundred meters (2,300 feet) underground, Jimmy and the other miners waited.

And waited.

And waited.

Will rescuers find the miners? Turn to page 48 to find out.

EPIC FAILS

ABOARD THE COSTA CONCORDIA cruise ship in 2012, Kathy Ledtke had just finished a breadstick and was looking forward to dinner when she felt a grinding thud. The lights flickered and went out. Even though an announcement told passengers it was simply an electrical problem, Kathy and her husband were worried. They headed for the lifeboats.

There, they were told to step back. Everything was fine.

But Kathy was right to worry. At 9:30 p.m., the vessel had smashed into a submerged rock off the Italian island of Giglio, ripping a hole wider than a football field through the steel hull.

Though the ship was soon tilting sharply, the crew told passengers (and officials on shore) that the situation was under control. Back inside the dining room, it was the serving staff—not the crew members—helping passengers don life jackets.

Finally, more than an hour after the crash, Captain Francesco Schettino gave the order to abandon ship. By that time, the angle of the vessel made it impossible to launch some of the lifeboats. Kathy and her husband made it into a boat, but many passengers were left clinging to the railings, waiting desperately for rescue helicopters. And some said that the captain wasn't there to help—he'd already fled to shore.

Thirty-two people died in the *Costa Concordia* disaster, and Captain Schettino was later charged with manslaughter.

In terms of emergency management, the wreck was a massive failure. But it was hardly the world's first. In 1872, a crisis in leadership that included a poisoned captain and an incompetent engineer left nineteen people stranded on an ice floe. One of those people was 8-year-old Punny Ebierbing.

ISLAND OF ICE

PUNNY WAS THE DAUGHTER of a famous Arctic guide named Tookoolito (Taqulittuq in her native Inuktitut). Tookoolito wasn't your average nineteenth-century Inuit woman. She'd traveled to London and met Queen Victoria. She was fluent in English and could read and write. She'd sailed the Arctic Ocean with explorer Charles Francis Hall, then journeyed south to the United States with him to raise funds for future expeditions.

In 1871, Captain Hall was determined to pinpoint the North Pole. So Tookoolito set sail again with her husband, Joe Ebierbing, and their 8-year-old daughter, Punny. This time, an Inuit family from Greenland was also on board—Hans and Merkut Hendrik and their three children, plus one more baby boy born on the voyage.

From the start, their ship, the *Polaris*, sailed into trouble. The ship had problems advancing through the thick fog and even thicker ice. The crew, from at least seven different countries, had trouble communicating and planning. And many sailors thought Captain Hall was a poor leader. In late October, after an expedition onto the Greenland ice, Hall fell seriously ill, ranting and delirious. He died on November 8, 1871.

Some members of the crew claimed the captain had suffered a stroke. Others, including Punny's parents, believed Hall had been poisoned. Hall himself had accused a few different crew members, including the ship's doctor, of this. And he may have been right—an autopsy many years later showed that Hall had swallowed arsenic before his death. But had it been given to him as a poison, or as an attempt at medication? At the time, arsenic was used for both purposes.

There was no way for Punny and her family to know for sure what had happened. But they missed him. Hall had always treated Punny as a particular favorite, and he'd worked with Tookoolito for many years. Suddenly, he was gone.

With sailing master Sidney Budington as their new leader, the crew continued north and spent most of a year trying in vain to reach the Pole. They finally turned to sail home in October 1872.

Each day, with ever-colder temperatures, the ice encroached closer around them. Then, during a particularly vicious winter storm, as water sloshed in the bottom of the ship, an engineer panicked. He ran through the vessel, shouting that the hull was breaking. And on hearing the news, the new captain yelled, "Throw everything on the ice!"

Frantically, sailors heaved supplies overboard. Some things landed safely; others fell on the cracked ice beside the ship and sank. Soon, people climbed from the vessel for safety, and to help organize the evacuation.

Punny was one of the ones who fled to the ice sheet, along with her mother and father. Assistant navigator George Tyson went with them. As he hauled one sealskin-wrapped package away from the grinding of the ship's hull, he found a couple of Hans's and Merkut's children tucked inside! A few minutes longer, and they might have been lost beneath the waves.

There was one other major problem: the engineer was wrong. The ship wasn't sinking. But when the ice suddenly cracked and split, the *Polaris* drifted away—leaving Punny and eighteen other people standing in the dark, pelted by blowing sleet. They were trapped on an ice floe, a floating island, surrounded by black Arctic waters.

Can Punny and her family escape the ice? If you need to know now, turn to page 43.

HANDS UP!

SNEAK UP BEHIND A FRIEND and shout. What does the fight or flight or freeze response look like from the outside? Your friend will crouch slightly, all limbs tense and ready. He'll clench his fists. And he'll freeze, assessing the threat.

Police and military forces around the world have tried training officers not to react this way. They've tried to create people so tough, so immune to stress and danger, that they would never flinch and never freeze.

It doesn't work.

These are such deeply ingrained reactions that we all flinch, no matter what our training. That's why police officers never keep their fingers on their gun triggers—if they're startled, and they automatically clench their hands, they don't want bullets flying.

What police officers and soldiers *can* do to deal with their fight or flight or freeze response is train their bodies and minds so that, after they flinch, they can react to danger as quickly as possible.

And that's what survivors have to do, too. They have to unfreeze. They have to set aside their initial fight or flight or freeze response, and start thinking about how to live through a longer period of danger.

Search and rescue professionals suggest that people lost in the wilderness force themselves to "STOP": Sit down, Think, Observe, and Plan. In other words, don't start running wildly through the trees, convinced you'll find the path around the next bend. Instead, admit that you're lost, slow down, and decide how to cope. Most search and rescue professionals also recommend that lost people stay in one place and wait for help.

But, for some people, the dangers of staying outweigh the dangers of leaving. Twelve-year-old Bala Nona and his family were born in a place where battling the wind and waves was part of daily life. When their boat's engine died in the Torres Strait—a body of water with many scattered islands between northern Australia and New Guinea—they knew that if they all stayed put, they would never survive. As they clung to their boat, they Thought, Observed, and Planned—and they made some difficult choices.

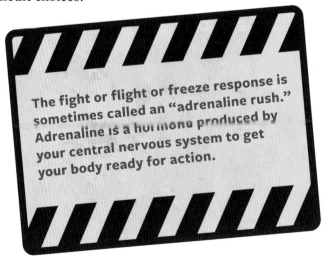

The fight or flight or freeze response is sometimes called an "adrenaline rush." Adrenaline is a hormone produced by your central nervous system to get your body ready for action.

STRANDED IN THE STRAIT

THE WAVES GREW. The motor died. With a lurch and a dip, the dinghy flipped, sending 12-year-old Bala Nona and his family plunging into the ocean swells.

They had set out from their Thursday Island home on July 6, 2004, heading to a relative's birthday party on a neighboring atoll. It should have been a four-hour trip. But halfway there, their motor sputtered to a stop. Then they couldn't control the dinghy in the rolling waves.

After the boat capsized, Bala clung to the hull with his 15-year-old sister, Ellis, and his 10-year-old sister, Norita. Bala's mom and dad kept little Clarence afloat; only 3 years old, he was too young to swim.

They tried and tried, but they couldn't get the dinghy right side up. So Bala's dad told the older children to swim for the nearest land. The waters were shark-infested. The tides could be treacherous. But Bala's dad was sure no one would search for the family—not for days. He was a church pastor, well known for stopping at distant islands and offering to help strangers. No one would worry if he were a few days late for the birthday party. With this in mind, he sent his three oldest children away from the boat and into the open sea.

"Don't worry about us—just swim," their mother told them.

So they swam. At first, they could look back and see their parents, clinging bravely to the boat. But after a while, they looked back and saw only waves. And even though they knew there was an island ahead of them, and the three were strong swimmers, their legs began to drag in the water. One hour passed, then two. No matter how hard they struggled, the current swept them aside.

When the girls grew tired, Bala told them they had no choice but to swim. "Keep up, or you'll get left behind," he said.

They prodded each other along until, finally, another shape grew in the distance.

It wasn't the island they had been hoping for, but they had found a rocky outcropping. Scraping their knees on the coral below, they dragged themselves onto the jagged black spire. There were only a few plants there, and no fresh water. As darkness fell, they found a sheltered spot amidst the stones, huddled together in their wet clothes, and tried to sleep.

What happens to Bala and his sisters when they wake up alone on a desert island? Turn to page 33 to find out.

EGO BOOSTS

THE MORE YOU KNOW, the better you can handle a problem. At Columbia University in New York, a professor named George Bonanno has spent years studying the people who are best able to cope with crises. And he found that these survivors often share a few traits:

- *a belief that they can influence events, and a willingness to learn from all sorts of situations*

- *confidence, or even overconfidence, in their own skills*

- *the ability to push emotions to the side, at least temporarily*

- *a talent for finding humor, or positive moments, even in the most stressful situations*

Bala had many of these characteristics. And so did the ancient traveler Xuanzang, centuries before . . .

SILK ROAD SURVIVAL

IN 629, the 27-year-old monk Xuanzang took a horse and set out from his home in China toward India, hoping to learn more about Buddhism by visiting its birthplace. His guide robbed and abandoned him in the middle of the Taklamakan Desert—one of the largest expanses of sand in the world. But although he had never attempted anything like this before, Xuanzang believed that he could make it across the desert by himself.

He wasn't as clever or careful as he thought he was. First, he wandered off course between the towers that marked his route.

Then, he accidentally spilled his water. But while he could have despaired as he watched the last of his fluid draining into the hot sand, instead he put his emotions aside. Xuanzang reminded himself that he had sworn an oath to reach the western edge of the desert or die trying. Despite the odds against him, he still felt confident.

After four days of staggering through gritty winds, he and his old horse lay on the sand, exhausted. It was a figure in a dream—a tall spirit encouraging him—that gave Xuanzang the strength to drag himself up, prod his horse back to standing, and continue.

On the fifth day, his horse tugged on the reins, turning in a new direction. The monk followed—and survived. The animal led the way to a desert oasis.

This near-death experience didn't dissuade Xuanzang. He traveled 16,000 kilometers (10,000 miles), met with kings, and scaled mountain ranges before he finally returned home. He became one of the most famous travelers and scholars of the ancient world.

FROM THE DAYS OF XUANZANG to those of modern survivor Bala Nona, some things remain the same. A crisis begins with moments of heart-thudding, lung-bursting fear. Our blood vessels squeeze, our pupils dilate, and our fists clench, ready for danger. No matter where or when we live, we're all programmed with the fight or flight or freeze response. We freeze like panicked squirrels, and many of us don't start moving again as quickly as we should. Fortunately, most of the people in *these* stories put their supersized human brains to use. They overcame their initial shock and they focused on finding their way to safety.

But overcoming your jumpy response is only the first step to survival. Next, you have to overcome hunger, or thirst, or freezing temperatures, or blazing sun, or a lack of oxygen. And the longer you're lost, the harder it becomes to stay alive . . .

CHAPTER 2

LIVING ON

THE EDGE

Humans aren't physically adapted for extreme environments. We don't have fur to keep us warm, or hooves to help us move over rough terrain. We need a constant supply of oxygen, regular food and water, and—ideally—access to shelter, clothes, even shoes.

On mountaintops, goats are better equipped than we are. Your average goldfish would fare better in the open ocean. And in a rainforest, an ant could out-survive us. We're high-maintenance creatures!

And yet, amazingly, humans have figured out how to make homes for themselves in all kinds of environments. They've terraced mountaintops, built skyscrapers in deserts, and even established an outpost in space.

Many survival stories end when lost or injured people are rescued by locals—those who understand the land best. If you're ever lost, or trapped, or stranded somewhere, the best strategy is to find people who know their way around!

UP, UP, AND AWAY!

IN DECEMBER 1920, three navy officers on a New York hot-air-balloon training flight were blown off course and ended up far to the north, near Hudson Bay. Though poorly dressed for the remote wilderness they landed in, they did have two carrier pigeons, a pocket knife, matches, and a compass. And one of them proved to have perfect luck lighting campfires in rough conditions.

After a chilly first night, the pilots cooked their pigeons. They ate one for breakfast and saved the other for dinner, but they found that a pigeon split by three men wasn't exactly filling. Between bird-meals, they hiked through trees, trees, and more trees, checking their compass to determine which way was north and then striving to hold a straight line, searching for signs of civilization.

After another night in the forest, and another day hiking, they began to lose both strength and hope. One lay down to die and would only start walking again when dragged to his feet by the others.

By day four, the men were faint with hunger, nauseated from unclean drinking water, and aching from cold and lack of sleep. Then—like a beacon—a pair of sled tracks appeared in the snow. They followed the tracks to the edge of a frozen lake and staggered across. When they spotted a human figure in the distance, they yelled and waved so wildly that the man took off running!

Eventually, Cree trapper Tom Marks understood their cries for help. He led the three balloonists to his cabin, where he shared his fire and the food he'd trapped. After that, he shepherded them to safety at the remote Hudson's Bay trading post in Moose Factory, Ontario.

The navy men would not have survived if they hadn't found someone with knowledge of the local environment to provide food and shelter. Then again, sometimes even locals get lost and need rescuing. We humans have a strange talent for leaving the safety of our white picket fences and getting ourselves into treacherous places.

Bala Nona lived in an isolated place. The islands where he grew up, in the Torres Strait off the coast of Australia, were home to far more sea creatures than humans. So once his family's birthday party trip went wrong, and they lost their boat, they found themselves in serious danger . . .

STRANDED IN THE STRAIT

BALA AND HIS SISTERS rose chilly and damp in the early-morning sun. And soon they were thirsty. The tiny outcrop they'd reached offered no fresh water or food, and they had no supplies. Though they were in the tropics, surrounded by ocean, they may as well have been lost in the desert.

That first day, Bala found a few oysters in the reef. They ate those, but the shellfish did nothing for their thirst. The rock they were perched on had no shade, and the sun beat down mercilessly.

Their only hope was for a fisherman to pass by in a boat. But although Torres Strait had more than 270 islands, only 14 were inhabited. Bala and his sisters knew that their chances of finding help were slim.

Over the next two days, the siblings put all their survival skills to use. Thanks to time spent with his fisherman uncle, Bala knew what was safe to eat and what wasn't. They nibbled more oysters, and he fished a floating coconut out of the sea and fed his sisters the milk.

By day three, though, their thirst was so severe that they couldn't resist swishing the seawater in their mouths. Though they knew they shouldn't, they drank a few swallows. That's when Bala decided they'd have to swim again. If they stayed on the rock, without fresh water, they'd die before anyone found them.

Now, if you were one of Bala's sisters, you might have needed a little convincing. After three days in the sun with little food or water, would you have the strength to swim? Would you worry about predators? Torres Strait is known for its healthy population of sharks, including Great Whites—creatures than can smell blood or urine in the water from five kilometers (three miles) away. And in the reefs surrounding many of the islands, crocodiles roam.

Despite the dangers, Bala was convinced that they needed to swim if they were going to survive.

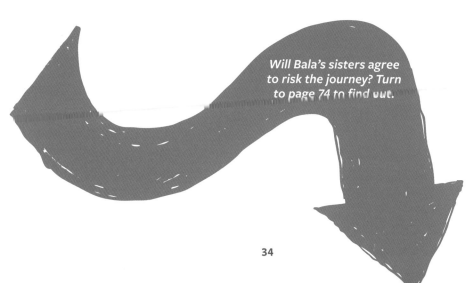

Will Bala's sisters agree to risk the journey? Turn to page 74 to find out.

DRY DAYS

MOST OF US DRINK 1.5 to 2 liters (6 to 8 cups) of water a day. But if you're hot (as you might be on a sunny day in the South Pacific, or an afternoon in the desert), you lose extra water through sweat. If you're stressed, you sweat even more. Workers in desert heat can lose 7.5 to 11 liters (2 to 3 gallons) a day, and soldiers in combat sometimes need twice that much—about five giant jugs of fluid.

Desert survivors can sometimes make do with less—if they're smart. In 1994, an Italian ultramarathoner named Mauro Prosperi got lost in a sandstorm while running a 233-kilometer (145-mile) race across the Moroccan Sahara. He conserved the scant fluid in his one water bottle, he drank his own urine and sipped dew from a few leaves, he ate bats and snakes, and he rested in the shade of an ancient mosque.

Mauro was an extreme athlete *and* a police officer—someone trained to deal with crises. And, at one point, even he gave up hope. Deciding that a quick death would be better than slowly slipping away in the desert heat, he tried to commit suicide by cutting his wrists. However, he was so dehydrated that his blood was thicker than normal and it clotted quickly. After nine days alone, Mauro was eventually found and rescued by a nomadic desert family.

Would you have been able to stay calm and think clearly for nine days under those conditions? What about a month? Two months? Four?

The race Mauro was attempting was difficult enough, even before he got lost! The Marathon des Sables is the length of six ordinary marathons. It's run over six days, and organizers provide only tents and water. Runners must carry everything else they need.

ALONE ON THE WAVES

CHINESE SAILOR POON LIM was working on board a British merchant ship in World War II when it was torpedoed by a German submarine. Surrounded by smoke, the deck listing beneath him, Poon Lim grabbed a life jacket and leapt into the ocean. He sank deep into an ooze of seawater and oil before his life jacket propelled him to the surface. There, he grabbed a wooden plank to keep himself steady while he scraped the oil from his eyes.

By the time he could see, the entire ship had disappeared beneath the waves. He heard a few shouts, but Poon couldn't swim. Knocked around in the rolling swells, he couldn't see anyone alive. Then the German submarine surfaced, pulled a lifeboat alongside, and took several members of Poon's crew as prisoners.

Poon begged to be captured as well, knowing he wouldn't survive the open sea. But the crew only mimed shooting at him, then laughed. He was left behind.

After the submarine disappeared, Poon fought for hours to reach an empty life raft. And there, he found supplies—water jugs, a few biscuit tins, chocolate, sugar, flares, smoke signals, and a flashlight. With these basics, he kept himself alive. He made a fish hook with a wire from his flashlight and another one from a nail in the raft. He soaked his life jacket each time it rained and drank the water he could squeeze out of the canvas. After his fresh water

supplies dwindled, he caught both a bird and a shark and drank blood to survive.

When fishers finally rescued Poon Lim off the coast of Brazil, he'd been alone for 133 days. That's the longest anyone has ever survived aboard a life raft.

CRAVING LIKE CRAZY

MORE THAN HUNGER, more than heat, it was thirst that plagued Poon Lim aboard his raft, a constant craving for something to drink. When you aren't taking in enough water, your body naturally prioritizes and decides which functions need the water most. Less water in your system means drier blood vessels and thicker blood, so to make sure you have enough pumping to your vital organs (brain, lungs, kidneys, etc.), your heart beats faster. Less blood goes to your extremities and to your skin, leaving your skin and eyes feeling as if they're shrinking and stretching. You grow mildly feverish.

If you don't get water quickly, your heartbeat grows irregular, your organs stop working, and less blood reaches your brain. Your thinking blurs. It becomes difficult to orient yourself or make plans. Basically, as you're dying of thirst, you'll discover it's more and more difficult to find water.

Once your body's in this sort of shock, you'd have to fall face-first into a puddle to survive. Which is pretty much what survivor Juliane Koepcke did. Water was the one problem she *didn't* have.

ALONE IN THE AMAZON

CAN YOU IMAGINE thinking about Christmas one minute, and crashing into the Amazon the next? When Juliane's plane splintered, it dropped her deep in the rainforest. She woke there in the morning, injured and alone.

Her head still foggy, Juliane searched in widening circles around her crash site. She found nothing more useful than a rain-soaked cake and a bag of hard candy. There were no signs of other survivors. Though she called and called, Juliane heard nothing. Little did she know that her mother and thirteen other people had also made it alive to the rainforest floor, though most were too injured to move.

Where Juliane had landed, the rainforest was hopelessly dense. There was no way for planes to see through the thick canopy above her, and there were no trails for rescuers to follow. Juliane was on her own. She was petrified that she'd lost her mother, but she wasn't scared of the rainforest itself. And she was confident she could survive it.

After all, Juliane had spent much of her childhood exploring her parents' nature preserve and she knew how to interpret the sounds of birds and frogs and rustling leaves. She also knew the sound of trickling water. For the first day, she slaked her thirst on water drops from leaves. On day two, she followed her ears to a tiny stream. Her zoologist father had taught Juliane that water always flows toward more water, and rivers always lead to human habitation.

Taking each step carefully, leading with her sandal-shod foot and watching for snakes, Juliane began hiking. She followed the slowly widening streambed until dark, then curled into a hollow in the bank and tried to sleep.

For days, Juliane continued walking downstream. She skirted a poisonous bird-eating spider. She clambered over rocks and logs that blocked her path. On the fourth day, she discovered the bodies of several other passengers. Forcing herself closer, she checked whether her mother was among them. But there was no familiar face. And while Juliane was horrified and saddened by the sight of the corpses, she was also grateful her mother wasn't there. She still hoped to find her mother alive.

Occasionally, Juliane saw or heard a search plane, but they were much too far away to signal. And every day, she grew a little weaker. Her tiny stash of hard candy was long gone and she was surviving on gulps of murky river water. She tried catching frogs, but she wasn't successful.

Wounds in her leg and shoulder grew infected. As the stream joined others and merged into a river, Juliane decided to float rather than walk downstream. Even though she worried about piranhas, and she could feel the sun blistering her skin, and she longed to curl up and sleep on the riverbank, she forced herself to continue.

The river was choked with logs and debris and there was certainly no sign of human life. Still, Juliane held on to her father's words: rivers lead to people.

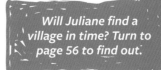
Will Juliane find a village in time? Turn to page 56 to find out.

TAKING THE HEAT

IN THE DEPTHS OF THE AMAZON, Juliane had a sundress and one sandal. Armed only with these tools, she had to face an environment that had defeated thousands of Spanish invaders and other foreign explorers. There were dangerous creatures, from jaguars and boa constrictors to poisonous frogs and flesh-eating fish. There were toxic plants and biting insects. And compared to those early explorers, Juliane was at a disadvantage. Historians believe that the Amazon rainforest was once home to millions of people. But by the 1970s only a few hundred thousand lived there, in isolated villages. It was going to be difficult for Juliane to find anyone who could help her.

Fortunately, a couple of circumstances were in her favor. First, she had plenty of water. Though its bacteria might eventually make her sick, she wouldn't have to deal with immediate dehydration. And Juliane was near the Equator. During the day, the temperature in the Amazon hovers around 27°C (80°F)—pretty much ideal for humans. When the air is about equal to human body temperature, we don't have to work too hard to stay cool or stay warm. In scientific terms, this is called the "thermal neutral zone." In a sundress, soaked by rain, Juliane would have been chilly during the dark nights, but not freezing.

Had Juliane crashed in a northern forest, she would have had to add new problems to her list. If temperatures drop below freezing, frostbite can damage or even kill tissues, usually in the hands and feet. Low temperatures can also slow your bodily functions and make you confused and uncoordinated. This condition is called hypothermia. As your body temperature drops below 28°C (82°F), your heart and other major organs can stop working. If you can't find a way to warm up again, you will die. Survivors who find themselves in colder climates need to find shelter—or rescue—even more urgently than those who find themselves in the Amazon.

A WILD EDUCATION

SOME OF THE WORLD'S top wilderness survival experts live and conduct their research in eastern Canada. There, a combination of large expanses of forest and plenty of outdoor recreation means—unfortunately—that hundreds of hikers and hunters get lost each year.

In Nova Scotia, a university professor named Kenneth Hill has studied the wilderness behavior of everyone from elderly deer hunters to small children. He's also examined the search methods used by police. One of the things he's discovered is that calm searchers and confused victims don't always see the forest in the same way. A toddler, for example, might curl up inside a log for shelter, and might be frightened by the sounds of men searching in the night. Even a lost adult can stumble haphazardly for hours, crossing into areas that have already been searched by orderly rescue teams.

To learn exactly how people react when they're lost and alone, another researcher went to unique extremes. Gino Ferri was an elementary school principal and a wilderness survival buff. He spent years researching thousands of northern Ontario search and rescue cases. Then he interviewed about a thousand survivors. And finally, he put his information to the test. For his PhD project, Gino got himself lost in the forest with no food, water, or matches. At one point, it took him seven hours to light a fire.

In Kenneth Hill's study of elderly deer hunters, he discovered that weaker memories and space-mapping abilities meant these hunters were more likely to wander and get lost. But because the hunters had already developed good wilderness skills, they tended to sort things out on their own and rarely needed rescuing.

Plagued by blackflies and sometimes reduced to eating bugs for supper, Gino was significantly thinner and much wiser when he emerged from the woods twenty-nine days later. He was also an undisputed expert on survival techniques.

The advice given by Gino, Kenneth, and many of Kenneth's deer-hunter study subjects is similar: stay calm, find shelter, and concentrate on the basics. But even when they're doing everything they can to stay safe, some people can't help imagining the worst. And others have to make difficult choices in order to live . . .

Fire-Starting 101: Gather dry leaves, grass, or bark. (This is your "tinder nest.") Next, find a stick about half a meter (two feet) long (your "spindle") and a relatively flat piece of wood (your "fireboard"). Put a notch in your fireboard and start rubbing your spindle back and forth—fast!—against the notch until the friction creates sparks. The goal is to make the sparks fall on your tinder nest so that it catches fire.

ISLAND OF ICE

THEY WERE STRANDED on an ice floe, their ship drifting away without them. Punny and her family had never imagined being left in a situation like this one. As they lost sight of the *Polaris*, Punny, her mom, Tookoolito, and her dad, Joe, wrapped themselves in musk ox skins and huddled together. Icy winds assaulted them from all sides, and by morning the family was covered in a thick blanket of snow.

Soon, the nineteen survivors gathered on the biggest ice chunk they could find and began building shelters. Under Joe's direction, everyone pitched in, leveling the ground and hacking blocks for the ice, eventually creating a small village of dome-shaped igloos. Though Punny and her mother knew how to light and heat their shelter with a blubber lamp made in a pemmican tin, it was difficult to teach the sailors. They kept setting the blubber on fire and smoking themselves out of their homes!

Meanwhile, the most senior crew member on the ice took stock of their supplies. George Tyson had traveled the Arctic for more than two decades. He knew what it would take to survive —though he thought their chances were extremely slim. The stranded sailors had fourteen cans of pemmican, eleven and a half bags of ship's bread, one can of dried applies, fourteen hams, and some chocolate. If they were trapped until the whaling ships came north in April, it wouldn't be nearly enough.

Thankfully, they also had guns, ammunition, two eight-person whaling boats, and two traditional kayaks. With those, the survivors could hunt.

If only the other crew members had listened to George. On the first day, cold and panicked, the men smashed one of the whaling boats for wood and built a roaring bonfire. Others broke into the food cache, feasting on precious supplies.

Joe and Hans went out every day to hunt for seals, but it wasn't sealing season. To find one, they had to lie on the ice for hours, motionless and watchful. Occasionally, rarely, they caught one. But even then Punny's belly wasn't full. The sailors refused to divide the meat evenly. Even though the Inuit men were the ones who caught the food, the white sailors considered the Inuit men beneath them and gave them smaller portions. Punny's meals were often a few strips of frozen entrails, or a piece of sealskin warmed over the lamp.

The stranded sailors set aside extra rations for Thanksgiving. That night, Punny and the *Polaris* crew had a "feast": a few sips of hot chocolate, two biscuits, and a couple of dried apple slices each, served with some seal entrails.

Punny's father said that he'd been in bad situations before, and endured winters with few supplies, but this was the worst hunger he'd ever experienced. Each day, the family grew weaker.

Punny's parents worried about darker things, too. If the Inuit men failed to find food, would the sailors eventually turn to other sources? If they got desperate enough to eat one another, as other Arctic expeditions had done in the past, Punny and her family worried that they could be first on the table.

There was one chance for escape. The two Inuit families could climb into the remaining whaling boat and try for the distant, ice-cloaked shore. They might make it and, once there, they might survive. But that would mean leaving all the other sailors to certain death. Without the hunting skills of Joe and Hans, the *Polaris* crew would have no hope.

So Punny and her family stayed. Some days, they resorted to chewing on sealskin meant for clothing repairs and eating the dregs of blubber from their lamp. Through December and January, as storms whipped over the ice sheet and wind howled around the igloos, they waited, worry and hunger gnawing within them.

Can Punny's father find enough food to last everyone through the winter? To find out, turn to page 69.

DESPERATE TIMES

LOST, STARVING, and even facing the threat of cannibalism, Punny's family chose to remain loyal to their fellow survivors. It may have been partly to support George Tyson. In his self-appointed leadership role, George had become their champion, advocate, and friend.

Whatever their reasons, the family stayed and continued to help feed the group through the long winter nights, doing almost all of the hunting and accepting unequal shares of the meat.

Survival situations don't always unfold so peacefully. Trapped far from civilization and facing desperate extremes, people begin to bend the rules of society. Just as castaways take tiny sips of sea-water to wet their mouths, then find themselves gulping down this poison, survivors can end up breaking one taboo, then another . . .

CROSSING THE LINE

IN 1846, the Donner Party, a group of eighty-one pioneers, set out from Springfield, Illinois, trying to reach California in a convoy of ox-drawn wagons. But the travelers eventually found themselves trapped in the Sierra Nevada mountains. The winter snows had arrived weeks earlier than usual, the group was follow-ing a new, unpredictable route, and the families were so attached to their wagons and supplies that they refused to abandon them, even if it meant getting stuck in the snow instead of successfully crossing the mountains on foot.

Somehow unable to work together, and trying to endure the winter in shoddy wood cabins and makeshift tents, the party soon ran out of food. They let many of their oxen wander off, to be buried in snow. And few of the would-be settlers had the

knowledge or energy to try hunting. By the beginning of December, they had nothing to eat but thin soups made of boiled ox hides, twigs, and bark.

Knowing they wouldn't make it through the winter in camp, fifteen of the strongest group members strapped on homemade snowshoes and tried one more time to cross through a mountain pass. They named their group "The Forlorn Hope." Soon, it began to snow. After several grueling days without food, the group discussed a horrible possibility: maybe one member should die, so the others could eat his body, and live. They even drew slips of paper. A middle-aged man named Patrick Dolan drew the unlucky piece.

But they couldn't do it. They couldn't kill him.

Then another storm hit. Huddled together, buried by snow, the members of The Forlorn Hope began to die, one after another. Three, then four. Patrick Dolan was one of the ones who didn't make it. Only then did the survivors cook and eat some of his flesh, as well as the flesh of the others who had died.

Of the fifteen members of The Forlorn Hope, seven made it to California. And by the time rescuers could reach the others, those trapped in the mountain pass had also resorted to eating the dead.

Only thirty-eight of the pioneers lived until spring.

Survivors can face excruciating choices. Save yourself or work to save everyone? Die or survive by cannibalism? For the members of the Donner Party and the crew of the *Polaris*, long winters of isolation brought depression, despair, and unthinkable alternatives.

THE BIG CHILL

AS DIFFICULT AS IT IS to survive in the Amazon rainforest, or on the islands of the Torres Strait, or in the Arctic, these are at least places where people *do* live.

What about the most extreme of Earth's environments—the towering glaciers that top our highest mountains, or the deep underground caves and crevasses? Humans have never lived in these places, and few are able to withstand them for long.

DEEP BENEATH THE EARTH

AFTER THE CAVE-IN trapped them more than 700 meters (2,300 feet) underground in Chile's San José mine, Jimmy Sanchez and his fellow workers found themselves with only an emergency cache of supplies. They had enough food to last two or three days, and they agreed to strict rations: tiny sips of milk, and a bit of tuna for each man every twenty-four hours. They managed to make their stores last for two weeks, though they felt themselves growing weaker.

When their food ran out, desperation set in.

By day seventeen, a few of the men had retreated to their blankets and refused to rise. They'd given up hope.

That's when the men heard the familiar sound of a drill. From far above them, rescuers were boring yet another hole through the rock, desperately looking for survivors.

Jimmy barely dared to hope. But when the drill bit burst through the rock and into their tunnel, he and the others were so excited they wanted to hug the metal. Instead, they attached a note.

When the drill rose from the earth, the rescuers read the words: "We are well in the shelter, the 33 of us." Though the workers above ground were supposed to wait for the Chilean president to fly in and make an official announcement, they couldn't bear to make families suffer any longer—they quickly spread the news that survivors had been found.

Above ground and below, hope was reborn.

That didn't mean the men were safe. To figure out how to reach them, the government flew in experts from around the world. With engineers, drilling specialists, and even NASA staff, they came up with a plan.

First, they brought in a drill that weighed about 30 tonnes (tons). Their plan was to bore a narrow channel through the rock, then slowly widen it until it was large enough for one man at a time to squeeze through. As the drill neared the refuge, making the walls shake, debris would shower into the tunnels, and the trapped miners would have to find the strength and courage to clear it away. The process would take months—some thought it would be Christmas before the rescue took place. And, after debating, the experts had to break that news to the miners below.

Jimmy, the youngest of the workers, was scared every single day. And when he slept, he dreamed of rescue. One night, he dreamed that his mom had walked into the mine to get him out.

Though that particular dream didn't come true, trapped mine electrician Edison Pena managed to wire a series of lights. Somehow, it made the tunnel seem just a little bit safer. And the miners at least had a new food supply. Through the original bore hole, doctors sent sugar water, then energy drinks, then finally solid food—the bare necessities of life, all dropped through the small tunnel in tiny packages the miners called *palomas*, or doves.

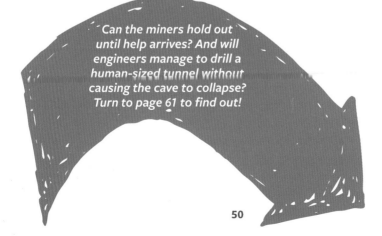

Can the miners hold out until help arrives? And will engineers manage to drill a human-sized tunnel without causing the cave to collapse? Turn to page 61 to find out!

Turn to page 61 to find out!

THE ULTIMATE EXTREME

THERE'S ONE PLACE more isolated than the bottom of a mine, and that's an environment explored by humans only for the last few decades: outer space. Not only is there no food or water in space, there's no air. Without protection, a human in space would die in less than two seconds.

In 1970, *Apollo 13* was launched and scheduled to land on the moon—the third manned space flight to make the trip. But before they got there, an oxygen tank exploded, damaging the capsule's Service Module. Suddenly, the crew faced limited power, a water shortage, and no way to remove dangerous carbon dioxide—all while they were 322,000 kilometers (200,000 miles) above the Earth.

Working with the command center far below, the astronauts began conserving supplies and making plans. When carbon dioxide rose to dangerous levels, they found a way to divert it using plastic bags, cardboard, and tape. To save their water supplies to cool the engines, they ate foods like hot dogs that were packaged in liquid. Finally, when the view from the capsule's windows was blocked by debris, making it difficult to steer the craft, the astronauts found a way to use the sun's position to navigate, and managed to point the capsule back toward its target destination. Then they used the moon's gravity to swing the vessel back toward Earth.

Usually, mission control had to wait only four minutes to hear from a crew dropping back through the atmosphere. This time, the four minutes passed in silence. Then another minute. And another.

Finally, sound burst through the radio. A voice. At mission control, dozens of NASA staff went wild.

Having survived zero gravity, limited oxygen, freezing temperatures, water shortages, equipment failures, and a searing plummet through the stratosphere, the three astronauts splashed safely into the Pacific Ocean, four days after the explosion.

HIGHS
AND
LOWS

LIKE THE OPEN OCEAN or alpine summits, space continues to tempt adventurers. Today, more than four decades after the *Apollo 13* mission, even civilians are training and paying to visit space.

We humans travel to the North and South poles, we brave the seas, we hike deep into forests and jungles. We explore the world's highest peaks and its darkest depths. Some people find themselves in these dangerous places because of their work. Others go by choice. They cross deserts and scale cliffs for the sake of learning, personal discovery, or pure adventure.

English mountaineer George Mallory was once asked why he wanted so badly to climb Mount Everest.

He said, "Because it's there." And sometimes, that's the best explanation people can give for wanting to tackle the planet's toughest challenges.

But George Mallory disappeared on one of his attempts to scale Earth's highest peak. His body was found seventy-five years later by another expedition. And eighteen astronauts and cosmonauts have died in space. No matter how long and how well people prepare for a journey to one of the world's inhospitable places, they can never fully account for all the dangers.

And, as some adventurers learn, sometimes the greatest dangers aren't lurking in the environment. Sometimes the greatest threats to your survival come from inside your own mind . . .

CHAPTER 3
BRAIN
GAMES

If you've ever run a long race or played a whole soccer game without snacks, or gone without a meal, you'll know that human thinking gets a little fuzzy without food. In a survival situation, deprivations are more extreme and can have much, much more serious consequences. First, people feel foggy. Then drunk. Then sleepy or apathetic or blank. Our brains divert fuel to the most crucial functions—things such as breathing, heart rate, and temperature control. Unfortunately, our brains don't consider complicated reasoning a crucial function!

THE CLOSER YOU GET to starvation, the harder it is to think straight, and the more difficult your problems become. When you add in dehydration, altitude sickness, insomnia, heat exhaustion, hypothermia, injury, or just a generous dose of stress, things can get even weirder.

You might think you see water in the midst of a desert. Or you might start talking to people who aren't really there. Or you might imagine you see rescue boats where none exist. Even if you manage to remember that you're supposed to keep your cool, fight panic, and focus on basic needs, these few simple things might start to seem impossible as the connections in your brain stop communicating.

In endless dark or relentless sun, enduring frigid snowstorms or crashing waves, the mind starts playing the strangest tricks—and, as Juliane Koepcke realized, sometimes the only thing you can do is to take back control by playing your own tricks . . .

ALONE IN THE AMAZON

BRUISED AND BATTERED by the plane crash, Juliane spent one day alone in the Amazon. Then a second. And a third. Cold, wet, and plagued by biting insects, she huddled against the river's gravel banks at night, or curled against the trunk of a tree, drifting in and out of fitful sleep. During the day, the sun baked her skin until her back felt crisp. And every night, she found herself weaker. It grew more and more difficult to drag herself over obstacles. More and more difficult to keep going.

When she'd first seen search planes, she'd felt hopeful. But as the planes stopped circling, she realized they'd called off the search for survivors. And while she knew that following her small river and looking for villages was the right thing to do, she could see that the river was so choked by logs and sandbars no

one would be bringing boats or canoes up the channel. At times, Juliane couldn't help feeling angry and hopeless. There were expanses of jungle on all sides of her, and no signs of human habitation. She was truly, terribly alone.

Still, she followed the river, clinging to the idea that the water would lead her to people. After a while her mind began to paint pictures and play sounds for her—she saw the roof of a hut among the trees, or heard the squawk of a chicken on the riverbank. Again and again, she raised her head to investigate, only to find that her senses were fooling her. Hut roofs became tree branches once more, and the chickens morphed back into rainforest birds.

But Juliane's imagination provided useful distractions, too. As she traveled, she began painting her own pictures, recreating her favorite meals in her mind. She built herself simple breakfasts or lavish banquets and imagined how good they would taste.

By this time, when Juliane touched her back, her hand came away bloody. Her skin had burned and cracked, peeling away in strips under the relentless sun.

WHEN JULIANE HEARD SOUNDS that weren't really there, she was experiencing a not-uncommon phenomenon. In one study, scientists interviewed people after they'd experienced high-pressure situations. About 3 percent said they'd heard a strange voice speaking to them. While some people heard reassuring words, others heard threats!

Either way, most researchers believe these hallucinations happen because the hormones released by stress can make our minds play tricks on us. And if you take intense stress and add oxygen deprivation, even stranger things can happen . . .

Can Juliane keep her head on straight under such grueling conditions? Turn to page 78 to find out!

CLIFF'S EDGE

IN 2006, CLIMBERS called Lincoln Hall's family from Mount Everest with terrible news. The Australian climber had died after summiting the mountain. As the altitude and lack of oxygen had caused his brain to swell, Lincoln had grown delirious. He had tried to climb back up the mountain. Other team members were forced to wrestle him to the ground and try to haul him down the ice. After several hours, Lincoln appeared lifeless, and the exhausted climbers left his body at the side of the trail and staggered back to camp.

But Lincoln was alive.

Somehow, he survived the night at 8,700 meters (28,500 feet) above sea level. The next day, an international climbing team found Hall sitting beside a 3,000-meter (10,000-foot) drop with his down jacket off, apparently unaware of the danger.

"I imagine you are surprised to see me here," he said (proving that the best survivors keep their sense of humor!).

Abandoning their own summit attempt, the climbers managed to carry the mostly blind and hallucinating man off the mountain.

Lincoln lost one toe and several fingertips to frostbite. Other than that, he was miraculously unscathed by his ordeal.

LINCOLN HALL WAS SUFFERING from a severe case of altitude sickness. That's a name mountaineers use for a group of conditions that can occur when people climb above 2,000 meters (6,500 feet). There, the air holds less oxygen. When people go too far, too fast, their brains start to swell and their lungs collect fluid. They can face coma and death if they don't get down the mountain soon enough.

Now that thousands of people are scaling the world's highest peaks, doctors have had lots of practice diagnosing and treating altitude sickness. But there are other conditions connected to surviving extreme environments that are still not fully understood. One of the most famous—or maybe infamous—of these conditions is called "polar madness."

POLAR MADNESS

FOR CENTURIES, as people strove to reach the North and South Poles, or find a passage through the Arctic ice, ships' captains wrote of mental illness plaguing the crews. Depression. Despair. Insomnia. Sailors experienced delusions, paranoia, and what came to be called "polar madness."

In 1898–99, the Belgian Antarctic Expedition was the very first crew to spend a winter locked in the ice around the South Pole. Months into their ordeal, the captain wrote: "The curtain of blackness which has fallen over the outer world of icy desolation has descended upon the inner world of our souls." Several sailors succumbed to mental illness; one died when he left his ship, determined to walk back to Belgium.

Today, long after the final reaches of Earth have been explored, scientists are still debating whether true "polar madness" exists. Many say the condition is simply a mix of responses to different kinds of stress. Yet research continues. And much of it takes place in Antarctica, where several countries run year-round research stations. That puts scientists and support workers in a land of ice, cold, and darkness for months at a time.

One of the first things researchers confirmed was that most people living in Antarctica experience insomnia—and it can have a strong impact on their sense of well-being and mental health. Even when they managed to nod off, research subjects never fell into deep, restorative sleep. They had fewer dreams, and they woke still feeling tired.

Humans have a sort of internal clock that keeps us sleeping at night and moving during the day. Because the North and South Poles have cycles of complete daylight during the summer months and complete darkness during the winter, people's internal clocks get skewed. Sleep becomes elusive. In more scientific terms, the disturbance in the cycle of light and darkness means the human body doesn't produce the right hormones. People experience insomnia, irritability, and depression. Even the brain's abilities begin to slow.

In terms of sunshine—or lack of sunshine—there are definite similarities between Antarctica and the depths of a mine. With the help of international experts, Jimmy Sanchez and the other trapped miners in Chile's San José mine had to find a way to regulate their sleep cycles. It was one of many ways they tried to keep their spirits up.

DEEP BENEATH THE EARTH

TO JIMMY and his fellow miners, rescue often seemed like an impossible dream. Though Chile's president promised to extract the trapped workers, and experts were working around the clock, the survivors were trapped in an unstable area. Every day, they walked the entire length of the tunnel, searching for cracks or signs of movement. Jimmy took on the role of environmental assistant, walking the refuge chamber with a tiny computer that allowed him to measure the oxygen supply. He relayed his findings to the medical team on the surface—so far, so good.

Jimmy and the other miners were still connected to the surface only via the tiny bore hole, through which they continued to receive supplies and pass messages. The drill that was supposed to make a tunnel large enough for people could dig only a few body lengths each day. If you took a skyscraper and turned it upside down in the earth, that's how far the drill still had to travel. Jimmy sometimes wondered if the drill would ever make it.

Above ground, rescuers brought in a consultant from NASA, the agency responsible for the American space program, to help address the miners' health concerns. After all, NASA had some experience with keeping people alive in confined spaces! Among other things, a medical officer named Michael Duncan suggested that the miners keep one area light and another dark, so the men could stick to similar, familiar sleep patterns. That would help the group continue to work together and would help them establish more restorative sleep cycles.

Underground, supervisor Luis Urzúa took the lead in implementing these suggestions. He also found other ways to help the men work together and think positively. He made sure many major decisions were made by democratic vote, so everyone had a say. To keep spirits up and the men moving, they set up teams of workers—some organizing the food, others clearing rubble or checking for any new problems.

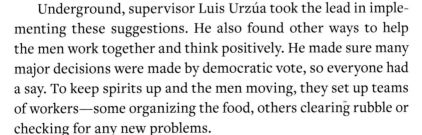

As the months passed, Jimmy struggled to stay confident that they'd one day be able to leave. Eventually, he found strength in his religious beliefs. "There are actually 34 of us here," he wrote in a letter to his father on the surface. "God has never left us down here."

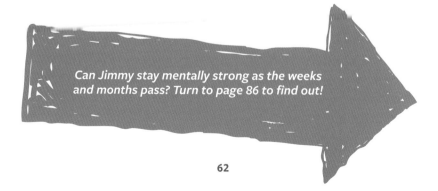

Can Jimmy stay mentally strong as the weeks and months pass? Turn to page 86 to find out!

POWERFUL WORDS

THE TINY CHUTE connecting the buried miners to the outside world was a lifeline—literally. Through it, rescuers sent food and medicine. And something equally important: hope.

Even though it interrupted the delivery of vital supplies, families were allowed to send messages through the bore hole. At first, psychologists asked people to write only positive news. But after a while, they were permitted to write about anything. To the men below, those letters were a link to normalcy. They kept hopes high through many dark and dreary days.

Hope is not easy for scientists to measure. But it's a key element to survival. Again and again, people claim they were able to endure terrible situations because they focused on family or home—they maintained hope that they'd eventually be reunited with the ones they loved.

That's something that doesn't always happen . . .

STRANDED ALONE

IN THE EARLY 1800s, violence broke out between the Nicoleño inhabitants of San Nicolas Island off the coast of California and groups of Russian and Aleut otter hunters who were hired to hunt in that profitable territory. By 1835, the otter hunters had left—but only a dozen Nicoleño people had survived the fighting.

When a Christian mission on the mainland heard of those people struggling alone on the island, they sent a rescue ship. An approaching storm may have disorganized the rescue efforts, though, because when the ship sailed away again, it took all the Nicoleños but one—it left Juana Maria behind.

For eighteen years, she lived alone on the island. She had a small cave for shelter and she built a rough whalebone hut near the beach. She managed to fish, hunt seals, and kill birds for their meat. She also made herself a dress out of the feathered skins of the birds she caught.

Juana Maria was "rescued" and brought to the Santa Barbara Mission in 1853. But by that time, she was the last Nicoleño person remaining in the world. Although she was finally living among other humans again, no one could understand her language. She died of dysentery only seven weeks later, possibly because her body wasn't used to the rich and plentiful food at the mission.

GOING SOLO

HOW DOES SOMEONE survive alone, without anyone to talk to, for years on end? You need to be able to make your own shelter, clothes, and food, but you also need to know how to manage your loneliness.

Intrigued by these questions, children's author Scott O'Dell wrote *The Island of the Blue Dolphins*. In this fictional account of Juana Maria's life, O'Dell imagines Juana Maria befriending and taming a wild dog for companionship. We don't know how the real woman handled her solitude. However, she is believed to have made markings on the walls of her cave. Archaeologists also think that she may have collected reminders of her family and friends. Excavations of Juana Maria's cave revealed two redwood boxes that contained more than two hundred shells, beads, hair pins, fish hooks, tools, and stones shaped to look like sea mammals.

GROUP WORK

JUANA MARIA was remarkable. It is very rare for someone to live for years without any human contact. For better or worse, many survival stories involve groups of people rather than isolated individuals. In these situations, communicating effectively and working together are key to survival. This starts from the earliest moments of the crisis, when we automatically check with the people around us. "Did you see that?" "Did you hear that?" "Should we run?"

In some situations, people's tendency to gather information can slow them down and delay escape. But in other cases, brains working together make better decisions. And in 2012, sailors in South Korea made a decision that many experts recommend: they chose to stay where they were, and waited for help to arrive.

When Typhoon Bolaven hit the Korean Peninsula, it shattered windows, uprooted trees, and toppled power poles. Along the coast of Jeju Island, the waves slammed two Chinese fishing vessels onto the rocks. Crew members fought to hold on as the storm shredded the large boats. And while a few braved the waves and tried to swim for shore, most gazed down at the wild water

and decided to stay put. Together, the men secured themselves as well as possible and waited, hoping for rescue.

Fortunately, the South Korean coast guard was on its way. But massive waves, pounding winds, and shallow waters made approaching the ships almost impossible. Risking their own lives, officers shot rescue ropes from the shore onto one of the smashed fishing vessels. Then, working hand over hand, they rode those rescue ropes over and through the waves until they reached the stranded sailors. Twelve men were guided to safety, and six other survivors were found on shore. At least five more sailors were killed by the storm.

When people are willing to work together, they often find they can achieve feats they never thought possible. And, as Dr. Jerri Nielsen discovered, that's the kind of thing that can happen when you find yourself with a life-threatening illness while stranded in a life-threatening environment . . .

MANY HEALING HANDS

IN 1998, while working for a year at a remote scientific research station at the South Pole, American doctor Jerri Nielsen discovered signs of breast cancer. It was the middle of winter, a time when it was impossible for planes to land on the ice. And there were no other doctors in Antarctica. What could she do to get through this crisis?

Jerri decided to use what she had—a crew of supporters ready to do just about anything to help. Using apples to practice on, she trained the base's welder to use a biopsy needle so a sample of tissue from her breast could be taken for diagnosis. Then, a mechanic helped Jerri prepare tiny glass slides for analysis, and a computer specialist turned the slides into images that could be sent via satellite to the United States.

When a military plane was on its way to air-drop equipment and medicine, even more crew members turned out to help, braving scarce oxygen and freezing temperatures to build marker fires, then collect the supplies, including chemotherapy drugs for Jerri. And five months later, when it was just barely warm enough for a rescue mission, an American nurse and crew volunteered for the risky Antarctic flight. They brought Jerri home for further surgeries.

Jerri eventually recovered, wrote a book, and worked as a motivational speaker, telling her story to crowds around the world. She kept cancer at bay until 2005, and she died in 2009.

PERSONAL SPACE

JERRI'S TENUOUS HEALTH meant her whole crew had to help save her. It was a triumph of teamwork. But often, people who are stranded together don't get along so well. Just imagine if you were locked in your classroom for months and months. Would certain people begin to bug you? Would a few students band together in separate groups, leaving others out? After a while, would you get sick of even your closest friends?

That's exactly what it can be like for people trapped on a lifeboat, in a space capsule, in a cave, or on an ice floe. When a survival situation stretches into days or weeks, group work is more than just collaborating on finding food, building shelters, and developing rescue strategies. It's also about dealing with other people's personalities. You have to deal with the same people day after day. You might be hungry or sick. And you have very little privacy.

In 1987, Russian cosmonauts Alexander Laveikin and Yuri Romanenko spent half a year together aboard a space station the size of a school bus. There were times when they wanted to punch something . . . or someone. But punching the one person you have to rely on to get you safely home from space isn't the best survival plan. They couldn't argue with one another. So Laveikin and Romanenko directed all their frustrations at the mission control people back on Earth! At one point, Romanenko grew so grumpy, he refused to talk on the radio any more.

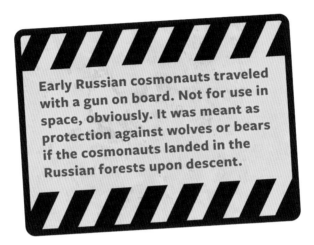

Early Russian cosmonauts traveled with a gun on board. Not for use in space, obviously. It was meant as protection against wolves or bears if the cosmonauts landed in the Russian forests upon descent.

ALEXANDER AND YURI both made it safely home, but astronauts who followed them agree that irritability can be a big problem on a long mission. On board the modern space station, crew members meet electronically each week with a psychologist, who monitors them for stress and instability. So far, there have been no nervous breakdowns in space.

Researchers who study people stuck in tight confines have found that the people who manage best are often those who can keep their emotions to themselves. Those who need to share everything, or people who are easily affected by the moods of others, have a harder time living in close quarters.

Of course, people are confident that their time at an Antarctic research station, or a space station, won't last forever. Early explorers weren't so sure. They could *hope* for a return to regular life. But always, there was the looming knowledge that their ship could be crushed in the ice. They could be lost forever.

ISLAND OF ICE

WITH THE POLARIS long-gone and supplies scarce, Punny and her family found themselves living day after dark day trapped on their icy island. As they floated slowly southward, the survivors had broken into three camps. A group of German sailors stuck together in one shelter. Hans, Merkut, and their children shared a second. And George Tyson—unable to understand the conversations of his German crewmates—chose to live in the third with Punny, Joe, and Tookoolito.

After weeks and months of strict rations, all of them were starving and cold, spending much of each day in bed to conserve warmth and calories. Punny was so hungry, the pangs made her cry. Inside their igloo, Tookoolito tried to distract her by telling story after story—some were adventures from her own life, and others were traditional tales from the Arctic.

The survivors dealt with their situation in different ways. For Punny's father, their plight meant long days hunting for food, then hunting again. He was relentless in his efforts. But he had the benefit of two sets of warm clothing. For George Tyson, going outside was almost impossible. All the sailors had tumbled onto the ice with limited winter clothing, but George had been wearing less than the others. He had barely enough to cover himself. He tried to do as much organizing and leading as possible from inside the shelter. Not that leading was easy. Some of the sailors were angry and unruly. Picking fights and stealing food from the community cache, they made many days both difficult and dangerous. Punny was sometimes scared of them, and she wasn't the only one. Both her dad and George started wearing guns for protection . . . just in case.

Hunger was still the greatest enemy. It was a constant struggle to keep the group from starvation. One night, Punny sat wrapped in a musk ox skin watching her parents play a makeshift game of checkers, with buttons for markers. She couldn't help

saying, every few minutes, "I am so hungry!" But nothing had been caught that week, there was no meat left to eat, and the checkers game continued.

One day, Punny was so bored that she dug knife-holes in the snow of the shelter, over and over again. It was no better in her friends' igloo, nearby. There, the oldest daughter chewed in vain on a piece of dry skin, holding a sick and malnourished toddler in her lap. The 4-year-old girl cried with hunger, and the baby lay languid in his mother's hood.

Sometimes, Punny could think of nothing except hunger and despair.

Will the Polaris survivors end up turning on each other? Turn to page 92 to find out.

CHOICES, CHOICES

EGGS OR CEREAL FOR BREAKFAST? Brown socks or white? Walk to school or bike? By the time lunch rolls around, you've already made hundreds of decisions. And with each of those choices, your brain burns glucose. To reason, plan, and decide, the brain needs fuel.

But what if your body has no fuel left? What if you've had nothing to eat for weeks? To function, we need at least a few calories each day—a bare minimum of 500 to 1,000, depending on our size. And in situations of extreme cold, like those faced by Punny's family or the Donner Party (page 46), our bodies burn energy ten times as quickly as usual.

WHEN WE HAVE no calorie intake at all, our body starts burning fat. After burning all the available fat, the body then uses its own muscles for fuel. Faced with starvation, men and young children don't last as long as women. This is because women store more fat in their bodies than men or kids. And men often burn protein more quickly and need to eat more in a day. Of the fifteen members of the Donner Party who hiked out to find help, eight of the ten men died, while all five women lived.

When you're starving, you will eat almost anything. You might even eat something poisonous—and that won't help clear your mind at all . . .

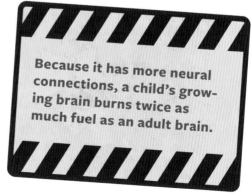

Because it has more neural connections, a child's growing brain burns twice as much fuel as an adult brain.

GONE SOUTH

THE AUSTRALASIAN ANTARCTIC EXPEDITION set out in 1910 to map the coastline of Antarctica and visit the South Magnetic Pole. In December 1912, leader Douglas Mawson—an English-Australian geologist—was riding a dogsled over an expanse of glacier. Belgrave Ninnis ran beside a second sled, while Xavier Mertz scouted ahead on skis.

At noon, when Douglas glanced back, Belgrave had disappeared. Where he'd been just moments before—a gaping crevasse. Six dogs, the food, and the tent were also lost. And though Douglas and Xavier spent five hours peering into the gap and calling for their companion, there was no answer from the darkness below.

The two explorers turned back toward base camp, forced to eat their sled dogs along the way. Soon, both were experiencing delusions, paranoia, and insomnia. Convinced that his fingers were frostbitten, Xavier chewed the tip off one of them. Then he flew into a violent fit and tried to destroy what basic shelter the men had left. He suffered seizures and hallucinations. What Douglas and Xavier didn't know: dog livers are poisonous. Their high levels of vitamin A can be toxic. When Xavier died on January 8, 1913, it was likely from a vitamin A overdose.

Douglas continued the trek by himself. At one point, he broke through the crust and slipped into another crevasse, saved only by his sled, which stuck haphazardly into the ice above. He finally dragged himself into camp, his feet too weak and raw to hold him, only to discover that his ship had departed. Douglas spent yet another winter on the ice, with a six-man search party who had stayed behind to look for him.

Despite its tragedies, the expedition had made significant advances in mapping, biology, magnetism, marine life, and meteorology. Douglas eventually made it back home, and was knighted for his achievements.

MIND CONTROL

IN THE MIDST OF crisis situations, there are few things people can control. Usually, they can't control their environments. They can't necessarily control all the equipment around them, the other people, or the arrival of rescuers. Worst of all, if they are starving—or experiencing food poisoning, or suffering from altitude sickness, or feeling delirious with fever—they may not even be in control of their own minds.

But those people who manage to successfully control their thoughts and reactions are the ones who are most likely to survive.

Bala, Norita, and Ellis Nona had no food, no water, and no strength left in their bodies. But Bala knew that if they were going to make it home, they were going to have to rely on what they did have: The will to push past their own physical limitations. The will to fight their despair. The will to live.

STRANDED IN THE STRAIT

THEIR BOAT WAS GONE. Their parents were gone. No rescuers had appeared on the horizon. Bala Nona and his sisters Ellis and Norita had been stranded for three days on a rock in the Torres Strait when they decided to swim for another island, hoping to find fresh water.

After judging the tides and working up his courage, Bala led the way back through the reefs.

Waves pushed the siblings into the sand and ground their hands and knees against the coral, but they dragged themselves onto another small outcropping, rested, then set off again for a third. In total, the children swam more than six kilometers (four miles). Staying close together in the waves, they fought against the currents and against their overwhelming fatigue. Bala alternated between encouraging his sisters and threatening them for their own good—telling them they'd be left behind or eaten by sharks if they didn't swim faster.

Finally, on the third island, they found food and drink. Bala easily recognized wongai, a local fruit that tasted like slightly sour dates. There were also coconuts—not the easiest food to eat, but the kids managed to tear the husks off with their teeth in order to drink the milk and eat the meat.

The fruit, along with seafood from the reef, was enough to fill their bellies. But without blankets or dry clothes, they were shivering by evening. And they knew that the little extra they had to eat wouldn't be enough to keep them going for very long. They also couldn't stop worrying about their parents, and little Clarence. Were they all right? Were they still clinging to the boat, or had they made it to an island too? Would they ever see each other again?

Hungry, thirsty, cold, and with no rescuers in sight, Bala, Norita, and Ellis had to wonder how long they could last.

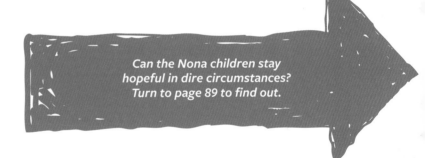

Can the Nona children stay hopeful in dire circumstances? Turn to page 89 to find out.

FOR SURVIVORS, mental challenges can be just as intense as physical ones. To live, people have to overcome their fears, concentrate fiercely on their needs and their plans, and stay hopeful in the face of overwhelming odds.

And then, just when they think they have everything under control, new dangers arise . . .

CHAPTER 4

BRAVING

THE WORST

You're hungry. You're thirsty. You're entirely alone. That's as bad as it can get, right?

Apparently not.

MOST OF THE PEOPLE in these survival stories faced terrible circumstances. And then things got worse. Just when they'd pushed their bodies beyond their limits, they were forced to face new kinds of danger. Animal attacks. Parasites. Diseases. Broken bones. Life-threatening infections. Blizzards. Rockslides.

More devastating than a danger itself can be your own reaction to it. If you experience too much fear, you might be paralyzed and fail to act to save yourself. If you experience a lot of fear over a long period of time, you might have trouble remembering things or making decisions. Your brain can even be permanently damaged.

So too much fear isn't good, but neither is complete fearlessness. In studies of athletes who compete in extreme sports, researchers found that a little bit of fear can help keep people alive. The pounding heart and gasping breath that come with a base jump or a tricky rock climbing move keep athletes alert; fear forces them to be cautious, and reminds them to be humble.

Fear might even help us in our everyday lives. Researchers at one university put absorbent pads in the armpits of people watching horror movies. Once those pads had soaked up some fear-scented sweat, other people sniffed them. Those other people were in the middle of writing a difficult test. And the ones who sniffed fear scored 6 percent better! Maybe, just maybe, thinking about a shark or worrying about wild animals can push us to think more clearly.

So, how can you use your fear to your advantage without letting it overwhelm you? Psychologists often recommend overcoming fears by facing them in a controlled way. If you're scared of heights, you might stand on a second-floor balcony one day, then a third-floor balcony the next. If you're scared of spiders, try looking at one from across the room. Then try standing next to its cage.

Obviously, none of this helps in a crisis. Survivors fear real dangers, and they don't have time for controlled experiments! They have to find different ways to manage anxiety. Some pray. Others chant, or repeat encouraging phrases to themselves. Distraction can help, too. People focused on helping loved ones or overcoming obstacles don't have time to worry about terror.

For plane-crash survivor Juliane Koepcke, thoughts of her mom needing help, or her mom and dad waiting for her, worrying, kept her constantly striving for survival.

ALONE IN THE AMAZON

JULIANE TRAVELED DOWNSTREAM for days through the Amazon rainforest, losing count of the nights she spent huddled in clouds of insects, listening for danger. Once, she heard pawing and hissing in the brush beside her. She cleared her throat loudly and the animal ran.

Other encounters were more dangerous. One day, she'd pulled herself onto a sunny sandbank in the middle of the current when something stirred beside her. She lifted her head to see a clutch of tiny caimans gazing at her, speckled eyes wide. Looking at the group of crocodile-like reptiles, Juliane knew she could be in trouble. Where there were baby caimans, there was a mother nearby, ready to protect her young. Then Juliane saw the creature, lumbering to its feet.

As quickly as she could, she pushed herself back into the current and swam away.

There were also dangers that Juliane couldn't see. She knew the waterways of the Amazon rainforest were home to venomous

stingrays, hiding in the mud, and sharp-toothed piranhas, feed-ing in the shallows. She tried to stay in the center of the current, where the fish were less likely to attack.

Of all the fears Juliane faced, the worst may have been beneath her own skin. On her shoulder and her leg, where she'd been badly sliced in the initial crash, flies had laid their eggs. Now, there were maggots burrowing deep into her tissues. She could see their squirming bodies. Removing a silver ring from her finger, Juliane bent it into a hook and tried to fish the larvae from her wounds. But whenever she got close to one, it wiggled deeper.

The maggots were horrifying, and they hurt, but Juliane told herself that she had no choice but to ignore them. She imagined her mother and father waiting for her, and she knew how wor-ried they must be. She also knew that there was a chance that her mother hadn't survived the crash. Although she didn't want to think about that, it drove her onwards. Her father would be devastated if he lost both his wife and his daughter. So she kept swimming, past all the wildlife dangers of the Amazon.

As Juliane continued downstream, she repeated her father's teaching over and over again: Rivers lead to people.

Rivers lead to people.

Rivers lead to people.

How long can Juliane maintain her focus and control her fear? Turn to page 110 to find out!
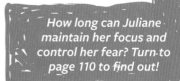

TALKING TO YOURSELF

THOUGH JULIANE DIDN'T KNOW IT, she was using one of the best strategies researchers have found to control fear and create focus. Scientists think that by chanting, using patterns, or breathing rhythmically we build a bridge between our conscious, thinking brain and the limbic system—the animal part of our brain that responds to fear. We're sending a message to our unconscious mind: we're in control, and things are going to be okay.

A British rescue team in 1974 decided prayer might be downright miraculous. They were called to Mount Kenya, Africa's second-highest mountain, a few days after a forest ranger there spotted a man heading for the peak. The man carried only a small bag of food and a piece of metal for shelter. He had no equipment and wore no shoes, but he insisted he was going to the top to pray to En-Gai, the mountain god worshiped by the Kikuyu people.

That's all the rescuers ever learned about the devoted climber. Five days later, as they were scaling the mountain to search for him, they spotted him heading back down a nearby ridge. Though they shouted, he chose not to stop. Instead, he continued barefoot through the treacherous mix of rock and snow. He seemed perfectly well—against all possible odds—as he came down the mountain.

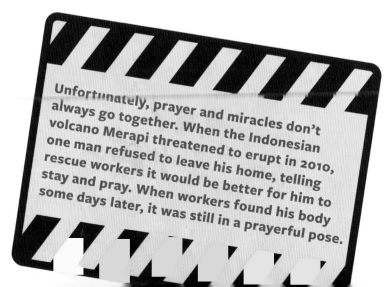

Unfortunately, prayer and miracles don't always go together. When the Indonesian volcano Merapi threatened to erupt in 2010, one man refused to leave his home, telling rescue workers it would be better for him to stay and pray. When workers found his body some days later, it was still in a prayerful pose.

Hand surgeon and mountaineer Kenneth Kamler also learned firsthand about the power of the subconscious, on the slopes of Mount Everest. He was the only doctor on the mountain when a Sherpa named Pasang fell into a crevasse, wedging his head in the ice. He was conscious when the other climbers pulled him out half an hour later, but he soon began to stumble and slur. As swelling and pressure built inside his skull, he lost consciousness. His breathing and pulse began to slow. Kenneth wasn't hopeful—even in a modern emergency ward, Pasang's chances of survival would have been slim.

Around Pasang's tent, other Sherpas began to chant. Low, rhythmic prayers echoed through the camp. All through the night, they chanted.

In the morning, the doctor was shocked to see that the swelling had receded. Pasang opened his eyes. And when he recovered enough to be flown from the mountain, Kenneth believed it may have been just as much because of the soothing and healing effects of the chanting as because of anything medicine had been able to accomplish. Indeed, there are entire fields of research dedicated to possible connections between health and traditional chanting or music: music therapy, sound therapy, and sonic healing are just a few.

SUPERHUMAN EFFORTS

SOMETIMES, fear in a crisis situation can bring on a rush of adrenaline that gives us the strength to go above and beyond our usual abilities. When Tom Boyle Jr., saw a car run over a cyclist in Tucson, Arizona, he leapt out of his truck to help. But the cyclist was pinned under the vehicle. Taking a deep breath and bracing his feet, Tom heaved the entire car off the ground and held it up for forty-five seconds while someone else pulled the victim free.

The biggest weight Tom had ever lifted at the gym was 317 kilograms (700 pounds). The car weighed over 1,000 kilograms (over 2,200 pounds)! Tilting the car took so much force, he shattered several teeth by grinding his jaw. And yet, under extreme pressure, Tom managed to exceed his own limits and save someone's life.

What if you had to save someone, or yourself? What if you had to crawl down a mountain with a broken leg? Could you do it?

END OF THE ROPE

WHEN BRITISH MOUNTAINEER Joe Simpson slipped on the icy slopes of Peru's Siula Grande, he shattered his leg. His climbing partner, Simon Yates, began to lower him, rope-length after rope-length, down the mountain. Then . . . another disaster. Joe slid over a ledge, dangling where he couldn't reach the ice face. Suddenly, the climbers couldn't see or hear one another. And Simon couldn't haul his partner back to safety.

The weight threatened to pull both of them from the cliff. Simon did the only thing he could: he cut the rope.

Joe fell forty-five stories, deep into a crevasse.

Miraculously, he survived, cushioned by layers of loose snow. But the type of environment where Joe found himself—the bottom of a crevasse, surrounded by ice—is not at all suitable for life. If you were trapped in those depths, here's what you'd be feeling:

- *numb, as your blood left your limbs and pooled in your core*

- *dizzy, as your blood pressure dropped and your heartbeats grew strange and erratic*

- *breathless, as your muscles slowed and your cough reflexes shut down*

- *confused, as your body temperature dropped and your brain slowed*

Trapped in the snow, you'd risk disorientation, amnesia, and coma. To save yourself, you'd have to act fast.

And Joe did. Following a glimmer of light at the end of the ice canyon, he scraped his way to the surface. Crawling his way over rough terrain, dragging his broken leg behind him, Joe headed down the mountain to meet Simon. It took him more than three days, but he was determined not to give up until he reached safety. Back in England, Joe needed six operations . . . and then he headed once again to the mountains.

RISKING EVERYTHING

WHY DO MOUNTAINEERS undertake activities that carry such a high risk of death? The athletes themselves often talk about the thrill of exertion, challenge, and accomplishment. While there's no one gene or personality trait scientists can point to, many have tried to find explanations for why some people go to extremes while other people play it safe.

- *Modern life has too many rules. I crave excitement!*
- *My climbing companions are like my tribe. We seek adventure together.*
- *I love being close to nature—the fresh air, the wildlife, the big open sky.*
- *Facing my fears gives me courage and humility.*
- *Survival is power. I feel great!*

There are also scientists who look at the ways our brains are made, and how stressful experiences affect our thinking. They believe that when we take a risk once, and live to celebrate, our minds learn to expect success. We begin to associate daring

stunts with a flush of good feelings. So by climbing one mountain, and succeeding, mountaineers create feedback loops within their heads: climbing equals success equals burst of happiness. Seeking that feeling, these adventurers climb higher and higher mountains.

Some researchers take this theory a step further. They suggest that people climb peaks— or throw themselves off bungee-jumping platforms, or barrel over mountain bike stunts, or snowmobile through avalanche-prone terrain— because evolution has programmed humans to love the thrill of the chase. If we were hunting for our food, we'd relish that burst of adrenaline that comes from huge exertion followed by a successful kill. According to these researchers, people embrace risk because of how we evolved over millions of years.

ANCIENT EXTREMES

ADRENALINE JUNKIES are nothing new. People have been risking their lives in order to have adventures and wonder at new sights for hundreds, perhaps even thousands of years.

Ibn Battuta was once the world's most famous traveler. In thirty years, he journeyed 120,000 kilometers (75,000 miles), from Morocco to China. He met with rulers of more than fifty nations.

In 1342, Muhammad bin Tughluq, sultan of Delhi, sent Battuta as an ambassador to China. Battuta set forth with slaves, attendants, and packhorses loaded with goods and money. But the sultan's lands were dangerous. Rebels attacked the caravan; Battuta's retinue was overtaken by a thousand riders and three thousand foot soldiers. Separated from the others, the traveler fell from his horse and found himself in the hands of his enemies.

The leader of the rebels ordered Battuta's execution, but then inexplicably changed his mind and released him. For seven days, Battuta picked his way through a swamp. He found a village, but the residents refused to help. A soldier stole his shirt. And finally, when he tried to use his shoe as a makeshift bucket, he lost it in the depths of a well. Fainting, dehydrated, and exhausted, Battuta was saved only when another traveler stumbled upon him.

None of these events—and not his previous run-ins with bandits, not even a shipwreck—would dissuade Battuta from his travels. He eventually wrote a memoir, called *A Gift to Those Who Contemplate the Wonders of Cities and the Marvels of Traveling*.

Like Xuanzang of ancient China, or the mountaineers of today, Battuta chose to travel. He chose to experience adventure, both its high points and its dangers. But no one chooses to work in an old, outdated mine for the sake of adventure. Most, like Jimmy Sanchez, brave the dark and the dust merely for the sake of a decent wage. They're willing to sacrifice days of sunlight to help support their families.

Which makes it doubly unfair when they find themselves trapped far beneath the surface.

DEEP BENEATH THE EARTH

LIKE THE OTHER STRANDED Chilean miners, Jimmy Sanchez spent his first underground weeks covered in a thick layer of grime. The constant dust and dirt combined with his sweat to create a crust on his skin. The men sent a letter up to the surface asking for soap, but even after they'd received some, they faced a number of health-related challenges.

Because there was so little air circulation in the tunnel, the miners were constantly damp and sticky. After several weeks, Jimmy's skin was covered in a pimply rash. Around him, the other men suffered the same. They had open sores and cankers inside their mouths. For some, the lack of clean food and water also made dental infections flare, causing constant pain.

The men moved their main camp to a slightly drier patch deeper inside the mine. Meanwhile, doctors tried to treat their ailments as well as they could without meeting their patients in person. They sent antibiotic creams down the chute, along with vaccinations for tetanus, diphtheria, the flu, and pneumonia. In such cramped quarters with limited medical access, a disease outbreak could easily be fatal.

But what worried Jimmy most was the possibility of another cave-in. Above ground, crews were working around the clock to bore a rescue route. The huge drill that engineers were using to widen the tunnel offered the men their best hope of escape—but it could also destabilize the rock and trigger a bigger collapse.

There was nothing the men could do except watch the walls carefully for signs of new instability. At the first sign of shaking, Jimmy planned to dive into the space where they'd first found the emergency cache. That was the safest place. Even then, he knew his chances of survival would be slim.

To distract themselves, the men gathered each afternoon for a prayer service led by one of the workers. Then Jimmy would write his letters home. Once, the rescuers were able to send down

a projector and a fiber-optic cable to broadcast a soccer game in the refuge—a huge treat for Jimmy, a longtime fan. He also weathered long, boring, and anxiety-filled days by focusing on what he'd do when he reached the surface. He'd have to visit the hospital briefly, he wrote to his family. Next, he wanted to go to the cathedral and thank God for his survival.

Will the tunnel cave in before the miners are rescued? Turn to page 100 to find out!

YOUR BRAIN ON FEAR

WHEN WE'RE UNDER extreme stress, just as when we experience the fight or flight or freeze response, our body makes chemical changes. One of those is the release of a steroid called cortisone. It can pump us full of energy and act as a natural pain-reliever—both useful functions in a crisis. But over days or weeks of stress, cortisone can interfere with the functioning of the brain. It makes it more difficult to remember things, for example, and harder to concentrate.

In Switzerland, researchers gathered thirty-six volunteers and gave them all a test: remember sixty words for twenty-four hours. They recorded the results. Then they gave the volunteers each a dose of cortisone, and a new set of words to memorize. At first, the volunteers could list their new words just fine. But a day later . . . much of the list had slipped away. With cortisone "stressing" their brains, the volunteers had lost some of their mental abilities.

In a crisis, just when we need to think clearly, it can be doubly difficult. Sometimes, we need something—or someone—extra. We need motivation to focus.

TOGETHER TROUBLE

WHAT IF YOU WERE LOST in the wilderness with an injured friend? You would probably do everything you could to help, even if it meant putting yourself at extra risk. And if you brought your friend water, or scared away wild animals, he would be more likely to survive.

Here's the surprising thing: *you* might be more likely to survive as well.

Survival expert John Leach has interviewed victims from around the world, and he's found that some of the people most likely to endure in survival situations are doctors and nurses. Not necessarily because they have more knowledge, but because they take responsibility for the people around them. They don't panic, freeze, or despair. Instead, they do their jobs.

Focusing on a specific role can be a powerful thing.

In his book *Survival Psychology*, John tells the true story of a fishing boat wrecked off the coast of Hawaii. After the boat sank, the ship's crew split into two groups. On one of the life rafts, the ship's third mate took charge. He set up a rotation so that someone was always scanning the sea. He rationed the food and

water, and had the raft mopped regularly to keep everyone dry.

On the other raft, the ship's captain gave few orders. He sank into despair.

After two weeks, the rafts were found by a rescue ship. The men under the third mate's leadership were able to climb on board the ship. The survivors on the other raft had to be hoisted on litters. The captain himself had died the day before.

The best leaders aren't always the people with the highest rank, or the most training. In the life rafts, the third mate did a better job than the captain when it came to overcoming fear and shepherding his companions. He was the one best able to take responsibility and focus on the tasks that needed to be done.

Off the coast of Australia, it was the middle sibling who took charge, keeping his older and younger sisters focused and hopeful . . .

STRANDED IN THE STRAIT

THREE, THEN FOUR NIGHTS had passed since their boat had flipped and they'd left their parents and little brother to brave the treacherous waters of Torres Strait. Bala, Ellis, and Norita knew their relatives would be searching for them. But they also knew that there were hundreds of islands to search. What if they dozed off and a boat passed by? What if rescuers didn't spot them perched on the rocks? They spent each day scanning the horizon, looking for the smallest speck of approaching hope.

Between stints gathering fruit and seafood, Bala stayed close to his sisters and tried his best to keep them optimistic. As they shivered through the long nights, he tried to distract them with tales he remembered from back home. The Islanders of the Torres Strait often share traditional tales and songs at special events

and gatherings. Like the storytellers he remembered, Bala chose to tell ancient tales—ghost stories that had been passed down from generation to generation. If his sisters saw a red ghoul, he said, it would kill them. A blue ghoul, on the other hand, might whisk them home.

 Most of the time, the three were convinced they'd get home eventually. They imagined their relatives scouring the islands, one by one. And if help didn't arrive, maybe they could swim from one atoll to another, all the way home.

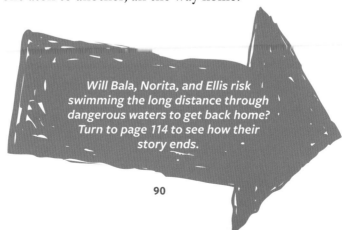

Will Bala, Norita, and Ellis risk swimming the long distance through dangerous waters to get back home? Turn to page 114 to see how their story ends.

As Bala mapped the islands in his mind, he knew they wouldn't have much of a chance. Still, he told his sisters it was an option.

He was determined to survive.

SOMETIMES, the need to save a friend or loved one keeps us going even when, alone, we might collapse in despair. Bala forced himself to stay positive and map out alternative scenarios for the sake of his sisters. In other situations, survivors have braved great personal danger to protect their companions.

THE ACCIDENTAL SAFARI

WILDLIFE ACTIVIST CARL DU PLESSIS was on board a small plane over Botswana's Kalahari Desert when the pilot reported an oil leak. Soon, the plane was pitching wildly, eventually crashing into a patch of trees and brush and bursting into flames. Carl was unharmed, but Lynette Nikolic, the only woman on board, had severe burns. Other passengers had broken ribs.

Along with pilot Costa Marcandonatos, Carl set off through the desert to find help. Leaving their one small bag of food with the injured woman and her two companions, the men stumbled over the searing-hot sand, using elephant paths to guide them. They found a muddy pool of water and dove in to cool themselves off. They heard lions roaring around them in the dark, but pressed on.

After four days and 200 kilometers (125 miles), they finally found a road. The two men were blistered from the sun and covered in mosquito bites when they finally stumbled into an army camp. But soon, they were guiding a search plane pilot to the crash site. All of the passengers survived.

AGAINST ALL ODDS

IMAGINE YOU'RE HUDDLED in the chilly desert night. You don't know where you are, you don't know how far you still have to walk. Then the lions roar.

For Carl, there must have been moments when survival seemed unlikely. But even when he thought he might become a midnight snack for giant cats, he managed to stay calm. And, like Carl, Bala and his sisters had to face their fears of starvation and thirst while clinging to life, hope, and the belief that, eventually, rescuers would arrive.

How much harder would it have been to hold on to hope while weeks, then months passed by? Punny and her family needed remarkable tenacity to stay committed to survival . . . even before the ice began melting beneath them.

ISLAND OF ICE

THE SURVIVORS OF THE POLARIS had lived on their ice floe for longer than they could have imagined. It seemed as if they'd been trapped forever. But as the ice drifted south and light slowly crept into the Arctic winter skies, Punny and her family began to find slightly more to eat. The men were so weak they had to work in teams to lift the boats, but Punny's father, Joe—by far the best hunter—managed to kill seals and seabirds in February, and then a massive elephant seal in March.

But the changing temperatures also brought danger. As the weather warmed, the ice began to crack. During one particularly violent storm, the entire ice sheet split into two, just steps from Punny's igloo. Punny shivered in fear, clinging to her mother as the pieces of ice smashed and slid against one another with ear-splitting crashes.

There was still no land in sight. On April 1, they crammed all nineteen people into a whale boat built for eight and rowed for a nearby ice patch that seemed thicker and stronger than their dwindling floe. But the boat was overloaded with people, skins, and sleeping gear. As the waves sloshed over the sides, Punny and the other children screamed and cried. In his journal, George Tyson wrote that he could hardly pull on the ropes without elbowing a frightened child.

Finally, they reached a more stable chunk of ice nearby. But they were left with makeshift canvas shelters and few supplies. Joe eventually managed to build a new igloo, only to have the ice break beneath it and carry it away. He built a second, and it split in two. With George, the family spent the rest of that night huddled by the boat, ready to climb aboard if the ice broke again.

A few days later, the ice cracked again just as breakfast was being spooned into bowls. While George and Punny's family survived, their breakfast was lost.

Then, as their floating island continued to bump and shear against other ice floes, another danger reached them. One of the men found a polar bear digging into the remains of a seal that Punny's father had recently caught. Punny saw her father rush into the shelter for his hunting supplies. They had little ammunition left, so he and Hans took their positions and waited until the bear came closer, closer. When they couldn't wait any longer,

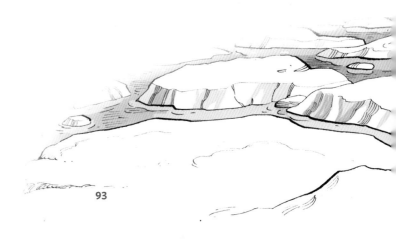

both fired. They managed to kill the animal. For the moment, their food shortages were over. But not the danger.

Every day brought new challenges. Waves crashed onto the ice, threatening to swamp each new camp or tear the boat from its moorings. With little shelter and steadily melting ice beneath them, the group struggled to hang on just until whaling season began, when the first rescue boats might appear on the horizon.

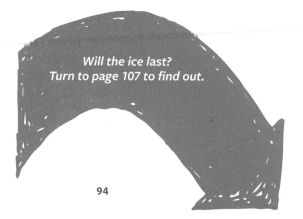

Will the ice last?
Turn to page 107 to find out.

KILLER SKILLS

ELEPHANT SEALS and polar bears. Storms and ice breaks. Would you know how to deal with such challenges? Could you climb aboard a whaling boat and bring home a seabird for dinner?

Probably not, and some of the sailors from the *Polaris* weren't much more skilled. They were saved by the local knowledge of Punny's parents and the other Inuit family on the ice. They alone understood the possible food sources and the creatures' habits. They knew how to lie unmoving on the ice, waiting for a seal to surface for air. They knew how to make lamps from seal oil, how to build homes from ice, and how to butcher a polar bear.

Without this indigenous knowledge, the crew of the *Polaris* would probably not have been able to navigate the dangers of the Arctic. To those men, Punny's family made all the difference between life and death.

SPACEWALK

THERE ARE SOME DANGERS that no one has the knowledge to negotiate. There are some places that will never be "local." Outer space, for example.

In 1965, Russian cosmonaut Alexey Arkhipovich Leonov was the first man to leave the relative safety of his spaceship and conduct a spacewalk. As his craft orbited the Earth, Alexey climbed from the *Voskhod 2*. Trusting the 4.5-meter (15-foot) safety line that tethered him to the hull, he let himself drift into the void. He crashed into the side of the spacecraft a few times. Then he attempted to "walk" along its edge, which felt like trying to move at the bottom of a swimming pool. After only twelve minutes he

was exhausted. But when he tried to climb back inside, he found that his suit had stiffened in response to the vacuum of space, and Alexey could no longer bend it through the portal. It was a problem no one had foreseen, because no one had yet stepped into actual space in only a spacesuit.

His heart racing, he tried going head first instead of feet first through the entry. That worked, but he couldn't close the hatch behind him, and he couldn't enter the main compartment of the ship until the outside hatch was closed! The cosmonaut struggled to find and release a valve on his suit. It would let the pressure escape, but he risked decompression sickness, or "the bends"—the same problem scuba divers face when surfacing too quickly. Gas bubbles could form in his bloodstream and might prove fatal. Alexey had to find just the right balance.

Fortunately, he did. He was able to squeeze himself—barely—to safety.

Although he had solved a problem that no human had ever faced before, Alexey's troubles weren't over. The automatic landing program on his shuttle malfunctioned and he and his fellow cosmonauts had to orient the craft themselves. After crash-landing in Siberia, they had to survive several days in the wilderness waiting for rescue. Although the temperatures were freezing and they had few supplies, they could at least breathe the air—and they knew that it wouldn't be long before they could be airlifted out.

THE WORLD'S SPACE AGENCIES have some of the most stringent training programs in history, and the most comprehensive emergency plans. But they can't foresee everything. That's because crises don't unfold according to a schedule, or a set of rules. That's what makes them crises! The stories of many survivors read like the twisting plotlines of action movies or suspense novels. And it's the people who can drive themselves forward even as danger looms who find themselves—sometimes, eventually—on their way home.

But if you thought getting home was the end of a survivor's story, think again. For many people, coming home can be the hardest part . . .

CHAPTER 5
THE OTHER SIDE OF SURVIVAL

News flash! Survivor rescued after weeks at sea! Injured snowboarder plucked from mountain cliffs! Pilot found after wilderness search!

When survival stories like these hit the headlines, the world tunes in. We stare at emergency wreckage on the news, or read the details on the Internet. Then we forget.

But what about the survivors? Can they forget?

ONCE THEY'VE FACED the planet's harshest physical and mental challenges, it can be difficult for people to return to regular lives. Imagine if you'd been stranded in a dark underground cave, surviving on only the tiniest bites of food and sips of water. How overwhelming would it feel to walk through the aisles of a grocery store, with rows and rows of colorfully packaged food? Or what if you'd been starving in the desert, and when you returned home you saw your little sister was refusing to eat the crusts of her sandwich? Would you feel angry? Grateful? Sickened? Confused? Survivors face all these emotions, and they must process them while feeling pressure from friends, family, and colleagues to return to their normal daily responsibilities. The media spotlight can add pressure as well. It can be a tough transition.

The three hot-air balloonists who were blown off course over northern Canada and trekked through the wilderness (page 31) were some of the first survivors to face a true media "circus." When New York reporters heard the men had been found, they flew to Ontario and raced on snowshoes and sleds to see who could meet the balloonists first and get the big scoop. One reporter actually camped with the men during their hike out from the trading post, then rushed back to prepare his report. But his feet blistered so badly he found it too painful to snowshoe, and he missed his train to the city. Talking to a different reporter, one of the balloonists made himself sound like a big hero, and implied that one of the other guys was a wimp! The two balloonists ended up in a fistfight on the train platform. It was all the stuff of reality drama—1920s style.

The Donner Party (page 46) also faced a media circus. Their tale of hardship and cannibalism quickly became legend. Newspapers reprinted their letters and diary entries in full. Tourism started up around the lake where they had camped, and buttons, nails, and cabin splinters from the site were sold as souvenirs.

For those members of the Donner Party who had survived, the extremes they had endured on their way to California took a deep toll. Some denied that cannibalism had ever happened. Others reported details, then later changed their stories. One woman refused to acknowledge that she was ever a part of the expedition, even when contacted by scientists and historians.

With the introduction of television cameras and twenty-four-hour news shows, media attention has only grown greater, and modern audiences are even more fascinated by survival stories . . . as the Chilean miners discovered in 2010.

 # DEEP BENEATH THE EARTH

AFTER THE MINERS MANAGED to attach a message to the drill bit telling the world they were still alive deep within the collapsed San José mine, it took another fifty-two days for rescue to finally arrive. Engineers had to plan and drill a twisting, sloping passage into the cavern, moving tons of rock along the way. During the final days, as the drill hammered above his head and the miners all wondered which day, exactly, it would break through, Jimmy could barely sleep. The anxiety made everyone edgy and irritable.

But once the drill had broken through, the tunnel had been reinforced, and the escape capsule was finally ready, the men didn't argue about who would be first to escape—they argued about who would be last. They were all willing to stay longer, just to make sure their fellow miners got out safely. In the end, the rescue team decided who would lead the way. They chose Florencio Avalos for his intelligence, his good health, and his experience underground. They chose the man least likely to panic while all alone in the cramped rescue capsule.

So in the early morning hours of October 13, paramedics descended into the cave to help extract the men. They dressed Florencio Avalos in a jumpsuit for the change from hot and humid underground cavern to cold desert night. And they trained a tiny video camera on him, to watch for signs of distress or nausea as he traveled to the surface—which, thankfully, didn't materialize.

As Florencio whooshed upward, Jimmy Sanchez watched him go, anxious with excitement, knowing it would be his turn soon. "I know that when it's my turn, nerves are going to hit with a vengeance," Jimmy had written to his family a few days before. "I have suffered enough down here and don't want to suffer any more. I hope that when it's my turn, everything will be okay."

Jimmy was the fifth miner to enter the chute, and, to his great relief, everything did go smoothly. For fifteen minutes, his capsule slid up the channel and he saw only rock. Then he was at the surface! He emerged to the welcoming faces of rescuers and the embraces of his family. Crowding in behind the families were two thousand journalists and camera operators, transmitting the scene to a billion viewers around the world.

Jimmy focused only on his family as he was guided to a stretcher and whisked to the temporary hospital set up on site, then eventually helicoptered to a larger hospital nearby.

Even after his hospital stay, Jimmy wouldn't tell the waiting reporters much about how he and his fellow workers had responded to their days in darkness. Together, they'd made a pact not to talk about their emotional struggles. Their motto seemed to be "What happens in the mine, stays in the mine." After supporting each other through days of hope and days of despair, they didn't want to tell stories about other people's weaknesses. Instead, they vowed to celebrate survival.

The final miner to ride the rescue capsule was foreman Luis Urzúa, the man whose calm leadership had helped all thirty-three miners withstand the ordeal. He was embraced at the surface by Chile's president, Sebastián Piñera, who said, "You're not the same after this and neither are we. We will never forget this."

IN THE SPOTLIGHT

JUST A FEW MONTHS before the cave-in, the thirty-three Chilean miners had been unknown to the world, working long shifts in harsh conditions for only $1,000 to $1,500 a month. Suddenly, they were famous. Producers offered movie deals, editors pitched book concepts, and David Letterman sent invitations to appear on *The Late Show*. While some of the workers seemed to revel in the attention—one even began charging journalists a set fee per question—others opted out of the spotlight, quietly returning to their families.

A Chilean businessman donated money to each surviving miner, and Jimmy used his funds to travel. But like most of the workers, he soon found himself in need of an ordinary job, and struggling to rebuild an ordinary life.

For some, that proved difficult. When *Time* magazine asked to interview one of the miners a year after the rescue, his wife said he was coping with complications of his mood medications and was not able to talk to the media. He wasn't alone. The majority of the miners had nightmares, emotional problems, and difficulties sleeping after their ordeal. A few suffered more serious symptoms of what doctors call Post-Traumatic Stress Disorder. One of the miners was filmed yelling at his family, asking why he had to die, even while they insisted that he *hadn't* died.

Post-Traumatic Stress Disorder can last for years, and symptoms include nightmares, feelings of isolation, guilt, anxiety, and phobias. For those who suffer the very worst symptoms, the lines between everyday life and survival situations grow blurred. Sometimes, a harmless activity can trigger memories so powerful that the person feels as though she is living through the life-threatening crisis all over again.

After the wreck of the *Trashman* and her ordeal in the life raft (page 15), it was a long time before Debbie Kiley ventured back into the ocean. One day, a year and a half after the incident,

103

Debbie's friend convinced her to go surfing. Debbie paddled out, only to struggle for air while waves hurled her against the sand. She couldn't right herself—and she couldn't remember why she'd ever loved the sea in the first place. As she dragged her body to shore, she found herself reliving the horrors of her five days at sea—the sharks, the hunger, the deaths of her companions. Debbie crawled crying into her friend's truck. Once home, she flew to her father's house, where she spent three weeks in bed. Only once she began writing and talking about her story did she finally find some relief.

For those who have suffered life-shattering crises like Debbie's, fear doesn't necessarily end with the arrival of a rescue ship. Terror can suddenly interrupt an ordinary grocery shop or a neighborhood drive. It's as if, after spending so long on red-alert, the human brain can't always return to its placid state.

Occasionally, a brain on high alert can be dangerous . . . for the survivor, and for others! Such was the case with Lieutenant Hiroo Onoda. World War II didn't end for this soldier until long after the rest of the world had moved on.

NEVER SURRENDER

JAPANESE INTELLIGENCE AGENT Lieutenant Hiroo Onoda and a small contingent of troops had been sent to Luband Island in the Philippines during World War II with these instructions: fight a guerrilla war in the jungle, no matter what happens, until you're picked up by the Japanese army

But when the Japanese surrendered, they forgot to tell Hiroo and his small cell of soldiers that the war was over. Messages sent by locals and pamphlets dropped from American planes announced the end of fighting, but these failed to convince the guerrillas. Hiroo thought enemies were trying to trick him.

From his hideout deep within the jungle, he and his soldiers kept fighting. They continued to sabotage "enemy" infrastructure and attack people in the area. Two of his fellow soldiers eventually "deserted" and returned to civilization, and two others were shot and killed by local authorities. Still, Hiroo battled alone, surviving without medical care or companionship, eating only bananas, coconuts, and the occasional stolen cow.

In 1974, nearly thirty years after the war had ended, a young Japanese student set off into the jungle, determined to find out whether Hiroo was still alive. He found him, and attempted to convince him that the world was at peace, something Hiroo refused to fully believe until his former commander—now a gray-haired civilian bookseller— flew to the island and relieved him of his duties.

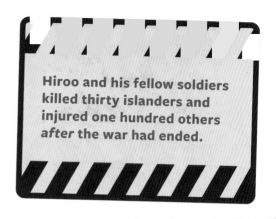

Hiroo and his fellow soldiers killed thirty islanders and injured one hundred others after the war had ended.

LASTING EFFECTS

POST-TRAUMATIC STRESS DISORDER can affect people who have endured a wide variety of circumstances, from car crashes to military battles. Research has shown that people susceptible to the illness have a smaller hippocampus at the base of their brain, and this reduces their ability to recover from shock. Scientists have also theorized that the disorder may have a genetic link. And sometimes, previous anxieties or mental illnesses can be magnified by survival situations.

Many survivors wind up in a therapist's office. And there, they often learn new coping strategies:

- *remember that bad times are temporary*
- *reach out to friends and family for help*
- *set new goals*
- *focus on the future*
- *pay attention to the things you do well*

Even for those survivors who don't suffer from Post-Traumatic Stress Disorder, and even with the best of coping strategies, the transition to ordinary life isn't easy. People still have to deal with harsh memories, decide whether their old careers or friends are still important to them, and, often, cope with lingering injuries or weakness. Weeks or months without proper food, water, and clothing can have a permanent effect on the human body.

Are some people born with smaller hippocampi, making them more susceptible to stress? Or does this part of the brain shrink under pressure? To find out, researchers studied sets of twins where one twin had been to war while the other stayed home. They found that hippocampus size is determined at birth, and not changed by experience.

ISLAND OF ICE

THEIR SUPPLIES SPENT, their bodies starved, and their Arctic ice floe melting around them, Punny and the other survivors of the failed *Polaris* expedition were clinging—both literally and figuratively—to life. One day, basking in a brief period of unexpected sunshine, Punny found herself staring at George.

"Why, you're nothing but bone!" she said.

And he agreed.

Then, on April 28, they spotted a steamer in the distance. It was too far away to contact, but it meant that the fishing season had begun, and the *Polaris* survivors had reached a part of the ocean traversed by vessels. Two days later, another boat appeared. This time, the men managed to leap into the whaling boat and chase after rescue, waving a flag and firing shots in the air.

For Punny, the wait must have been agonizing as messages were sent and a rescue ship organized. She must have watched with excitement—and maybe a little fear—as the brave captain of the *Tigress* carefully nosed his ship through the shifting,

unpredictable ice. Then Punny and her mom climbed into one of the ship's small seal-boats, while the men of the *Polaris* paddled their own boat toward the steamer.

It was official—they were saved.

The *Tigress* didn't turn immediately for shore. Instead, the crew continued their seal hunting. But the rescued sailors were washed and fed, the captain was kind to them, and Punny probably felt the same way her friend George did as he wrote in his journal: "Never in my life did I enjoy a meal like that . . . I shall never forget that codfish and potatoes."

But the rescue was only part of the recovery. Now that the immediate danger had passed, Punny and her family found themselves with bad colds and swollen feet and legs, the result of months of exposure.

And when the group arrived in St. John's, Newfoundland, on May 12, Punny faced exposure of a different sort. Crowds of people who'd heard the story of the *Polaris* gathered to see the children who'd managed to live through such harsh conditions. Soon, Punny had new clothes, more friends than she wanted, and more cake and candy than she could eat. After a diet of plain seal meat, all the sugar made her sick.

Then . . . it was back to normal for Punny.

But what was normal?

Hans, Merkut, and their children returned to Greenland. Punny and her family went first to Maine, and then to Connecticut, where her father owned a small house. He thought he could earn a living there by fishing.

Soon, though, he missed the Arctic. Joe chose to return north and continue guiding while Tookoolito stayed in New England with Punny. The little girl's health was never the same after her time on the ice—her body had been permanently weakened. In 1875, less than two years after her rescue, she died of tuberculosis. Though Joe tried again to convince his wife to travel north with him, Tookoolito refused. She lived for the rest of her life near Punny's grave.

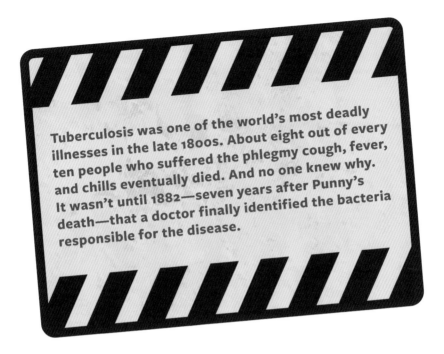

Tuberculosis was one of the world's most deadly illnesses in the late 1800s. About eight out of every ten people who suffered the phlegmy cough, fever, and chills eventually died. And no one knew why. It wasn't until 1882—seven years after Punny's death—that a doctor finally identified the bacteria responsible for the disease.

BOUNCING BACK

WHAT DOES IT MEAN TO RECOVER? If your daughter dies and you choose to live far from your husband and homeland, are you still suffering, or have you returned to a "normal" life? Many survivors ask themselves similar questions. *What is normal? What should it be? Why have I lived when others have died, and what can I do to make the rest of my days worthwhile?*

A crisis situation can force people to assess and evaluate and perhaps make drastic changes. But many survivors do manage to patch their old lives together again. To scientists, this is known as resilience. That's a fancy word for what most of us know as "what doesn't kill you makes you stronger."

It's true that people must face many challenges after living through a crisis. But many—*most*, actually—manage to overcome the shock. Some even pursue new ideas about how to live, or how to change the world . . .

ALONE IN THE AMAZON

PLANE-CRASH SURVIVOR Juliane had been hiking through the rainforest for so long, and her mind had been playing tricks on her for so many days, she didn't believe her eyes when she first noticed the shape on the riverbank. But when she looked again, it was still there. She drew closer, and the shape remained.

She found a small boat tied to the bank. Nearby was an unoccupied hunter's shack.

 Crawling inside, Juliane found a container of gasoline. She unscrewed the cap and poured the gas on her wounds, flushing some of the maggots out. Then she curled up on the floor to rest.

 That's where three forest workers found her. At first, they didn't know how to make sense of what they were seeing—they thought she might be a spirit from the river. When she spoke, and they discovered she was a victim from the plane crash ten days before, the story seemed almost as unlikely.

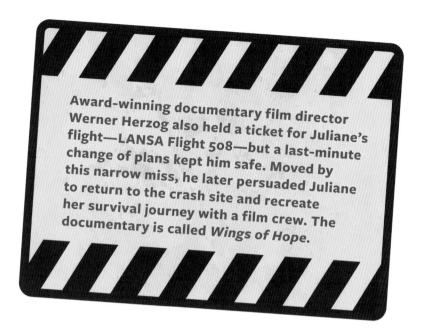

Award-winning documentary film director Werner Herzog also held a ticket for Juliane's flight—LANSA Flight 508—but a last-minute change of plans kept him safe. Moved by this narrow miss, he later persuaded Juliane to return to the crash site and recreate her survival journey with a film crew. The documentary is called *Wings of Hope*.

Nonetheless, they ferried Juliane along the isolated river until it met another waterway. There, finally, was a village. A nurse patched her wounds and a local pilot flew her to a missionary outpost where she was met by doctors. A message was sent to Juliane's father, and Juliane learned disturbing news—all the other passengers on her flight, including Juliane's mother, were dead.

The world would have understood if Juliane had left the rainforest and never returned. People would have understood if she'd refused to fly ever again. Instead, she chose to pursue a career in conservation and help save the land her parents had loved.

In 1998, when she was already a well-known biologist, she went back to the rainforest to film a documentary about her experience. And a few years after that, she returned to Peru to establish a nature preserve, Panguana, where her parents' research station had once operated.

Despite the tortures she had endured and despite the devastation of her family, Juliane didn't try to forget her ordeal. Instead, she took her life's pain and turned it into her life's purpose.

NEVER AGAIN

LIKE JULIANE, many survivors spend time advocating for new policies and safety measures to help prevent future disasters. After the world watched the rescue of Jimmy Sanchez and his fellow miners, the Chilean government implemented new labor rules and safety standards. Just a year after the collapse, mining accidents in Chile had dropped by more than 50 percent.

After the *Costa Concordia* cruise ship sank off the coast of Italy in 2012 (page 20), survivors helped cruise associations form three new safety rules: extra life jackets on board, so that even if passengers aren't in their designated zones they can still find safety equipment; a limit to the number of people on the bridge, so the ship's captain can concentrate; and route plans that are known to all senior crew members, so that a sudden off-course move can be easily recognized.

Of course, no matter how many positive changes arise in the aftermath of disaster, most people would prefer that such crises were avoided in the first place.

SEARCHING FOR SURVIVORS

AFTER DECADES SPENT RESEARCHING emergency situations, some experts have devised formulas to explain how disasters occur. At the National Outdoor Leadership School in Wyoming, for example, they point to a combination of bad conditions, unsafe acts, and poor judgment. A storm, a badly maintained plane, and a sleepy pilot can equal a plane crash.

A blizzard, a poorly tied rope, and a risky, adrenaline-fueled climbing maneuver can lead to instant death.

The experts hope that by deriving such formulas, they can help people avoid specific risk factors.

Unfortunately, pinpointing reasons for disaster is easier than finding the perfect recipe for survival. But we know there are a few things that certainly help:

 Connecting with local people as soon as possible, or relying on others who know the local environment

 Focusing on the basics of water, food, and shelter

 Making plans and taking action

 Knowing your environment, and having some basic survival skills

 Having confidence, motivation, and intelligence— the more the better

 Relying on faith, chanting, patterns, or rhythmic breathing to keep you calm

 Getting along well with other survivors and caring for those who are injured or struggling

FOR SOMEONE WHO HAS LOST a family member, the road back to a normal life can be doubly hard. Some, like Juliane, try to accomplish something good, possibly in memory of their loved ones. Others seek the refuge of home, the comfort of good friends and relatives, and the promise of better days to come.

STRANDED IN THE STRAIT

FOR SIX DAYS after their boat capsized, Bala, Ellis, and Norita had been alone on the barren islands of Torres Strait, eking scanty provisions of food and water from the rocks. From the start, Bala had been the leader of their shrunken family. He arranged their days and rationed the food, and worked to keep his sisters' spirits high.

Finally, on Monday, July 12, hope appeared—a growing speck on the horizon. The children's uncle motored toward the rock.

He was one of a large group of islanders who had set off in boats the day before after realizing that the Nona family had never appeared at their birthday party destination. Now, on the tiny atoll, he found his nephew and nieces waiting.

Back home on Thursday Island, the three kids had to adjust to life without their parents. Their mom, dad, and baby Clarence were never found. But Bala found refuge in school, and in time spent fishing with his uncle. He and his sisters also received medals for bravery from the Thursday Island Council and the governor of Queensland.

Bala had spent many childhood days learning about fishing and "bush tucker"—traditional foods. Those skills had ultimately been crucial to him and to his sisters. For Bala's family and his fellow islanders, his survival was a sign that traditional knowledge was still vital in a quickly modernizing world.

PUNNY EBIERBING, Jimmy Sanchez, Bala Nona, and Juliane Koepcke were lucky enough to live through the crises that rocked their lives. Their stories were vastly different. Punny's family lived a century before Juliane. Bala and Jimmy lived on opposite sides of the globe. They faced different challenges—from burning sunlight to endless darkness, from Arctic chills to tropical heat, from isolation to insomnia, from dehydration to starvation. There was no perfect formula for enduring the challenges they faced. Still, they shared many important survivor characteristics, showing confidence and courage throughout their ordeals. Each survivor found a way to cling to hope, even in the midst of devastating trauma. Each used skill and knowledge to plan, act, and persevere. And each one was committed, above all, to life.

CONCLUSION

PUSHING
BOUNDARIES

Today, it's possible to take a GPS reading from the center of the Amazon rainforest. Make a phone call from the North Pole. Even tweet from the summit of Mount Everest. It's more difficult than ever before to lose yourself on planet Earth.

In some survival situations, this makes all the difference. If Punny had been born a hundred years later, her family would never have had to wait for six months on the ice. An emergency call would have gone out from the *Polaris*, directing search helicopters. With flares or searchlights or infrared cameras, rescuers would have pinpointed the survivors and swept them to safety.

But even with the most modern technologies, not all survival situations can be solved so quickly. In Chile, the government called in experts from around the world. Even NASA personnel arrived to help. And still, it took more than two months to extract the miners from their underground trap.

And not everyone has access to such technology and expertise. Juliane, who found herself in the jungle with nothing but a sundress and a sandal, had only her own skills to rely upon. And on the other side of the world, in their sparsely inhabited ocean world, the Nona kids relied on traditional knowledge to keep themselves safe.

With or without smartphones and portable GPS units, crises will always occur. Humans may not get lost on the ice as easily as they used to, but we still push ourselves to the outer limits of the planet . . . and beyond. As long as people continue to adventure and explore, there will always be risks. There will always be the chance that, someday, we will find ourselves in peril, and we'll need to survive.

ENCAPSULATED

It takes a spacecraft more than a year to reach Mars. If humans take that journey, will they arrive both healthy and sane? In 2010, six volunteers climbed into a 72-square-meter (775-square-foot) faux rocket, the *Mars500*, to find out. They faced hours of boredom, private spaces barely big enough to turn around in, and months of eating freeze-dried cubes of food.

Outside the simulator, scientists regularly tested the volunteers' blood and urine, ran psychological tests, and observed their behavior through countless cameras. Everything was done to make the men feel as if they were in space—even e-mails were delivered only after a seventeen-minute delay.

Previous, slightly shorter simulations had ended badly. During one experiment, the astronauts had managed to smuggle in alcohol, and things had gone quickly downhill. But the *Mars500* experiment was a success. The volunteers completed a simulated Mars landing and "returned" to Earth, seemingly unscathed.

Next: the real journey to Mars—and beyond?—begins . . .

FURTHER READING

Belanger, Jeff. *What It's Like to Climb Mount Everest, Blast Off into Space, Survive a Tornado, and Other Extraordinary Stories*. New York: Sterling, 2011.

January, Brendan. *Amazing Explorers*. New York: John Wiley & Sons, 2001.

Leroe, Ellen. *Disaster! Three Real-Life Stories of Survival*. New York: Hyperion, 2000.

Long, Denise. *Survivor Kid: A Practical Guide to Wilderness Survival*. Chicago: Chicago Review Press, 2011.

Ross, Stewart. *Into the Unknown: How Great Explorers Found Their Way By Land, Sea, and Air*. Boston: Candlewick Press, 2011.

Wishinsky, Frieda. *Explorers Who Made It or Died Trying*. Toronto: Scholastic Canada, 2011.

SELECTED SOURCES

Baxter, Barry. "Pair find help after four-day walk through Kalahari Desert." *National Post,* March 8, 2000, p. A11.

Blake, E. Vale. *Arctic Experiences: Containing Capt. George E. Tyson's Wonderful Drift on the Ice-Floe.* New York: Harper, 1874.

Blum, Deborah. "Finding strength: How to overcome anything." *Psychology Today,* May/Jun 1998, pp. 32–38.

Bonanno, George A. "Loss, Trauma, and Human Resilience." *American Psychologist,* January 2004, pp. 20–28.

"Brain Function: Rice University study shows scent of fear impacts cognitive performance." *World Disease Weekly,* April 25, 2006, p. 181.

Bremner, J. Douglas. "Does stress damage the brain?" *Biological Psychiatry,* April 1999, pp. 797–805.

Brymer, Eric and Robert Schweitzer. "Extreme sports are good for your health." *Journal of Health Psychology,* April 2013, pp. 477–87.

Bullis, Douglas and Norman MacDonald. "From Riches to Rags." *Saudi Aramco World,* July/August 2000, pp. 16–27.

"Camp Notes." *The Washington Post,* June 6, 1943, p. B2.

Carroll, Rory and Jonathan Franklin. "Chile Miners." *The Guardian,* October 14, 2010.

"Castaways." *Sixty Minutes.* MSN. August 1, 2004. Television.

Davis, Robert Allan. "The Big Chill: Accidental Hypothermia." *American Journal of Nursing,* January 2012, pp. 38–46.

Erickson, Kristine, Wayne Drevets, and Jay Schulkin. "Glucocorticoid regulation of diverse cognitive functions in normal and pathological emotional states." *Neuroscience and Biobehavioral Reviews,* 2003, pp. 233–46.

Fiscor, Steve. "Rescuers Work to Free Chilean Miners." *Engineering and Mining Journal,* October 2010, p. 24, 26.

Franklin, Jonathan. *33 Men.* New York: G. P. Putnam's Sons, 2011.

Franklin, Jonathan. "An underground city of fear, boredom and joy." *The Irish Times,* September 11, 2010, p. 11.

"God has never left us." *America,* November 1, 2010, p. 4.

Gonzales, Laurence. *Deep Survival.* New York: W.W. Norton and Company, 2003.

Jones, Gavin and Antonio Denti. "Captain of wrecked Italian cruise ship facing manslaughter charges." *National Post,* January 15, 2012.

Kamler, Kenneth. *Surviving the Extremes.* New York: Penguin Books, 2004.

Kassel, Matthew. "Shipwreck." *Business Insider,* January 19, 2012.

Kiley, Deborah Scaling and Meg Noonan. *Albatross.* Boston: Houghton Mifflin Company, 1994.

Koepcke, Juliane. *When I Fell From the Sky.* Green Bay: Title Town Publishing, 2011.

Krupp, E .C. "Hanging by a Thread." *Sky and Telescope,* June 2006, p. 43.

Leach, John. *Survival Psychology.* New York: New York University Press, 1994.

Madigan, Michael. "Plucky sibling survivors honoured for their bravery." *The Courier Mail*, September 10, 2005, p. 7.

Madigan, Michael. "Traditional skills saved castaways." *The Courier Mail*, July 17, 2004, p. 5.

Madigan, Michael, and Richard Finnila. "Miracle survival at sea—Brave kids endure six days alone." *The Courier Mail*, July 19, 2004, p. 1.

McCunn, Ruthanne Lum. *Sole Survivor.* Boston: Beacon Press, 1985.

Morton, Paul M. and Peter Kummerfeldt. "Wilderness Survival." *Emergency Medicine Clinics of North America*, May 2004, pp. 475–509.

Nickerson, Sheila. *Midnight to the North.* New York: Jeremy P. Tarcher/Putnam, 2002.

Palinkas, Lawrence A. "The psychology of isolated and confined environments." *American Psychologist*, May 2003, pp. 353–63.

Petrou, Michael. "Voices from Underground." *Maclean's*, November 10, 2010, pp. 40–44.

"Prayerful Climber Apparently Makes a Safe Descent." *The Washington Post*, August 23, 1979, p. A22.

"Return of the Lost Fighter." *Time International* (Canada Edition), March 6, 1996, p. 10.

Ripley, Amanda. *The Unthinkable.* New York: Crown Publishers, 2008.

Roldan, Moises. "Faces of 33 trapped men." *The Daily Telegraph*, September 2, 2010.

"Searcher finds no sign of life at crash scene in Peruvian jungle." *The Globe and Mail*, January 7, 1972, p. 35.

Sherwood, Ben. *The Survivors Club.* New York: Grand Central Publishing, 2009.

Simpson, Joe. *Touching the Void.* London: Vintage, 1988.

"South Korean typhoon: coast guards battle to rescue stricken ship." From the website of *The Telegraph*, accessed July 18, 2013. http://www.telegraph.co.uk/news/worldnews/asia/southkorea/9503651/South-Korea-typhoon-coast-guards-battle-to-rescue-stricken-ship.html

Stafford, Ned. "Jerri Nielsen." *British Medical Journal*, August 8, 2009, p. 347.

"Survivor offers secrets." *The Vancouver Sun*, February 5, 1990. A10.

"Tense final hours ahead for trapped miners." *The Times-Transcript*, October 11, 2010, p. C1.

Thomas, Lauren J., Sophie O'Ferrall, and Antoinette Caird-Daley. *Evacuation Commands for Optimal Passenger Management.* Australian Transport Safety Bureau, April 2006.

Weber, Bruce. "Lincoln Hall, Climber Who Survived Everest, Dies at 56." *The New York Times*, March 24, 2012, A28.

Wieners, Brad. "Making the Cut." *Outside*, January 2, 2004, p. 20.

Wise, Jeff. *Extreme Fear: The Science of Your Mind in Danger.* New York: Palgrave MacMillan, 2009.

Wriggins, Sally Hovey. *Xuanzang.* Boulder: Westview Press, 1996.

INDEX

ABOUT THE AUTHOR

TANYA LLOYD KYI is one of those people who freezes during a crisis. You should never rely on her to provide medical aid. Or even to call for medical aid. However, if you're ever stranded on a desert island and you'd like to hear some stories to pass the time, she will happily oblige.

Tanya is the author of more than a dozen books for children and young adults, including some about other scary subjects: *50 Burning Questions*, *50 Poisonous Questions*, and *50 Underwear Questions*. (And if you don't think underwear is a scary subject, you should see some of the contraptions in that book.) Tanya lives with her husband and two children in Vancouver, British Columbia.

ABOUT THE ILLUSTRATOR

DAVID PARKINS is the award-winning illustrator of well over fifty children's books. He has been a freelance illustrator since leaving art college in 1978. His work has appeared in school textbooks, as well as children's comics such as *The Dandy* and *The Beano*. His newspaper work includes editorial cartoons for *The Guardian* and *The Globe and Mail*, as well as strip cartoons for the *Toronto Star*. He has also produced editorial illustrations for, among others, *The Economist*, *The Walrus* and *Bloomberg Businessweek*. David lives near Kingston, Ontario, with his family.